HOLY CROSS

Holy Cross

A Personal Experience

Aidan Troy

CURRACH PRESS

First published in 2005 by
CURRACH PRESS
55A Spruce Avenue, Stillorgan Industrial Park, Blackrock, Co Dublin

www.currach.ie

Cover by Liam Furlong
Cover photograph by Pacemaker Press International
Index by Therese Carrick
Origination by Currach Press
Printed by ColourBooks Ltd, Dublin

ISBN 1-85607-922-8

CONTENTS

Dedication

To the Board of Governors of Holy Cross Primary School, 2001

PREFACE

THIS BOOK IS written not to hurt but to heal. It is no more than my perception of what happened on Ardoyne Road in 2001. Those events had a profound impact on all who were part of them. The protestor as well as the child going to school was affected by what took place.

The challenge now is for us to find a way of ensuring that all children will be safe and free from harm. When one child is under threat, it is an attack on all children. That is why the story of Holy Cross is of interest far and wide.

The heart of the story is the children. They are the heroes. They did nothing wrong. They never became bitter and they forgave. They showed what the Kingdom of God is like.

Healing for adults takes longer. It is still the challenge and the hope. This book is a contribution to speaking the truth in love. It is an invitation to an honest dialogue out of which a new hope may be born.

Michael Brennan of The Columba Press met me one day in a Belfast bookshop and sowed the seed of this book. He introduced me to Brian Lynch of Currach Press and all showed immense patience as this 'novice' writer attempted to tell an amazing story.

Many people who heard of the book project gave me the most amazing encouragement. For this I am most grateful. Sally Anne McInerney typed the first draft of the book and succeeded in reading my writing.

Kate Hayes offered to read the text, correct it and made some most helpful suggestions. Without her painstaking work the book would never have seen the light of day. To her husband, Michael, and her family for their patience during this work my sincere thanks.

Finally, the goodness of God in allowing me to serve such courageous and wonderful children will remain with me as a gift I will never forget. Celibacy remains an issue but I have been blessed with such special children.

Aidan Troy CP
Holy Cross
Ardoyne
Belfast
2005

CHAPTER ONE

THIS BOOK COULD not have been written if I had not gone through what became known as the Holy Cross School protest. It is born of a series of events affecting two groups of people living alongside each other. As the events happened, their effects – short and long term – could not have been foreseen. The full story will never be told – not because others before me have not recounted the events or that I will hold back; it can't be told because what happened is deeper than words. No telling of the story of the Holy Cross protest can adequately convey the events on Ardoyne Road, Belfast, in 2001.

This book does not tell the full story for another reason. It is written from the perspective of the children and their bewilderment as they went to and from school over a period of months. While not claiming to be the children's account of the events it is written with them principally in mind. Their parents have shared so much of their children's stories with me in many and various ways. It is a privilege to commit this account to paper.

This book is not written to demonise the protestors or to rekindle the tragedy of those months. The truth as seen by the children has to be told if we are to arrive at a point of being able to reach out to each other across the divide that sadly still exists. If this book gives us all a chance to revisit the Holy Cross School protest with the aim of finding forgiveness and peace, it will have been worthwhile.

Several people witnessing a road accident will all have seen the same event but the stories that emerge in the retelling of that same event will be different for each witness. This is one retelling of part of this story and makes no claim to be the whole truth. It is an honest and sincere effort to tell the story of 225 courageous children who wanted to go to school and were told that this was not possible unless they went off in a different direction instead of taking a short straight walk.

Ardoyne has featured in the news especially over the past three-and-a-half decades. It is a small nationalist enclave surrounded by loyalist communities in a patchwork of 'Orange' and 'Green' that is North Belfast.

Holy Cross is the name of a parish established in North Belfast in 1869. Three Passionists went to establish a monastery and church there. They belonged to the Passionist Congregation founded in Italy in 1720 by Saint Paul of the Cross. He had a dream of linking the 'crucified' of this world with the Crucified Christ in order to offer a message of hope and light in the face of despair and darkness.

A central aim of this new group of priests and brothers was to work constantly for Church unity. It was a Passionist, Blessed Dominic Barberi, who received Cardinal John Henry Newman into the Catholic Church on 9 October 1845. Having crossed the Alps, the Passionists spread throughout the rest of Europe and arrived in Ireland in 1856 when Mount Argus was established in Harold's Cross, Dublin.

Strangely for those days Bishop Dorrian asked the Passionists to establish a parish in this area of North Belfast. It was only in the late 1960s that religious congregations were asked to take care of parishes which were generally cared for by diocesan priests.

Thus began an association between the people of Ardoyne, the Diocese of Down and Connor, and the Passionists. Through world wars, riots, burnings, as well as in good times, the Passionists drew ever closer to their people. The history of the people of Ardoyne is inextricably linked with the Passionists.

As a parish, Holy Cross has lost many people through violence over the decades. Between 1969 and 1998, Holy Cross parish saw ninety-nine of its people killed in a violent way. A fascinating book, *Ardoyne The Untold Truth*, compiled by the Ardoyne Commemoration

Project, was published in August 2002. It has been made into a video/DVD and has proved hugely popular.

With the ceasefires and the Good Friday Agreement of 1998, people in Ardoyne, along with people of good will elsewhere, dared to hope that peace would finally come to a troubled and divided community. All appeared to be going well, and parents began to believe that their children would never know anything of the hatred and violence they themselves had gone through.

Poor housing, high unemployment and health problems would all be addressed once peace took hold. Everyone knew that it would take time but at least a start had been made. Some wondered if the positive situation was too good to be true. 19 June 2001 was to prove them right. That was the day when lines were drawn that would have a profound and far-reaching affect on children and adults alike.

I first saw Ardoyne in 1968. At that time, I was a Passionist student in Dublin. Every Thursday, there was a low-cost excursion train from Dublin to Belfast. A fellow student and I skipped classes one Thursday morning and made a journey into the unknown. We had heard so much about Ardoyne and the parish of Holy Cross that we risked taking a trip to see the place.

Neither of us had ever been in Belfast before and we spent a magical day there. We went to Smithfield to look at the market stalls, took a bus to Holy Cross via the Shankill Road, being careful to use 'English' money to pay the fare. We were fascinated by the accents of the people on the bus and in the shops. We even had enough money to have a meal before we took the train back to Dublin. Unfortunately, we were missed by the director of students. Little did I think that, over thirty years later, my life would be changed by events at Holy Cross!

My decision to see if my future lay with this group called the Passionists arose at the end my secondary education in 1963 at Christian Brothers in Bray. I had attended the CBS primary school in Greystones. My winning a Wicklow County Council scholarship relieved greatly the financial demands on my parents. On finishing secondary school, I set off for the Passionist novitiate at The Graan, Enniskillen, County Fermanagh, thus crossing the border for the first time.

In many ways, I was taking quite a risk in seeking to join a group whose principal work was preaching. As a child, I had suffered from a severe stammer. Even though it gradually passed, I was always nervous when having to speak in front of others. I dreaded having to say anything in class. Reading in church was a cause of huge anxiety to me as a student. To this day, I am conscious of a feeling of anxiety before speaking in public.

The year in Enniskillen wasn't easy and was not meant to be. During it, my faith in God was severely tested when my mother died unexpectedly after I had been there just six months. It was considered unusual in those circumstances to be allowed home for a parent's funeral. I was allowed to come home for one night, accompanied by the priest in charge.

The months that followed were as tough as any I have spent. Loss, confusion and the decision to stay or give up weighed heavily. One of the few consolations was that I knew that my vocation was not a 'mother's vocation'. It must have been equally hard for my father, brother and sister at home.

It would be another six months before I was allowed to see them again. They travelled to Enniskillen along with other relatives to witness me taking my vows as a Passionist on 27 September 1964.

After taking vows of chastity, poverty, obedience and a fourth one – to keep alive the memory of Christ's Passion – I moved to Mount Argus, Harold's Cross, Dublin, for studies at University College Dublin. I still carried the pain of loss in my heart and, truthfully, do to this day.

The university was in Earlsfort Terrace where the National Concert Hall is now situated. We cycled there each day along with many other seminarians. One group of sisters would arrive each morning by chauffeur-driven car.

Those three years at UCD were wonderful. As students, we were required to wear 'Roman collars' and, by direction of Archbishop McQuaid, every cleric and clerical student had to wear a hat! At 19 years of age, I both felt and looked foolish dressed like that. The hat was conveniently 'lost' at the first opportunity.

The study of philosophy, logic and psychology opened up a whole world of exploration and interest. There were exams to sit and eventually a Bachelor of Arts degree was achieved. The days of the abundance of vocations to the priesthood and religious life was to decline in a remarkable way very quickly. I did not know what lay around the corner. I did, however, know that the life and practices we were asked to live as students could not continue for students of the future.

The Second Vatican Council (1962–65) had encouraged an engagement of the church with the modern world. When, from 1967 until 1971, I studied theology at Clonliffe College, Dublin, there were models of the church opened up to us that were not yet within our experience. It was a time filled with hope and belief in the future.

Crimes of sexual or physical abuse and other clerical and religious scandals were never spoken about. Of course, as we know now, such abuses were always there and were occurring during that time but were covered up for the sake of preserving the institution. Appearances mattered more than truth. Once a student was present for morning prayer or night office and was seen at meals and other duties, little else was asked.

We had student meetings to try to introduce what we saw as legitimate change. I can recall one meeting where the priest in charge covered his eyes while a vote was being taken, in case he would see what way a student voted. What he didn't see need not worry him.

The study of theology and all its various parts brought its own challenges and insights. The lectures varied from excellent to poor. The professor of Scripture, the late Monsignor John Greehy, gave me a life-long love of the Word of God. He would frequently come into class with the daily paper and the Bible. He told us that the Word of God cast light on daily events, and daily events were a continuing revelation of God among his people.

In Clonliffe, Fr John O'Connell gave us a foundation in theology that helped us see the church as people of God rather than a hierarchy in charge of people. Years later, I was to come to know him as parish priest of Bray. He has never ceased to explore what the Spirit is saying to the church today. There were other inspirational and encouraging professors in those days of preparation for ordination.

The preparation we received in the late 1960s could not have envisaged the church and world in which we would minister during the next thirty years. While our intellectual formation was excellent, our personal development and ministerial training left a lot to be desired.

In 1967, at the age of 21, I made a final commitment to the Passionists. I did so freely and without pressure. But at no stage had I been psychologically assessed. In fact, shortly after final profession, our class of students was sent for assessment.

Ordination day was 19 December 1970 in the chapel of St Patrick's Teacher Training College in Drumcondra, Dublin. This was a wonderful day for the family, relatives and guests who surrounded me. The absence of my mother was keenly felt that day.

In June 1971, following final theological exams, I arrived in London to help out for the summer in Harlesden, north London, while the priests there took their holidays. It was my first taste of the real world, and the many years of study now had to come into play. That summer was a great learning experience. One day, when I was going into a ward at a local hospital, I was told that the women, including Catholics, were awaiting abortions. It was a new world.

Toward the end of that summer, I was assigned to the Passionist monastery in Crossgar, County Down. Internment had just been introduced in August of that year and Belfast had become a violent place. My work was to recruit vocations. This brought me to schools and colleges all over Ireland.

I can remember learning the roads in and out of Belfast. My problem came when I was diverted by police or military and found myself in areas where I may not have been welcome. Visits to schools and families in Derry gave me first-hand experience of places like the Bogside and Creggan.

While in Belfast during those years, I frequently called and sometimes stayed at Holy Cross. I saw something of the tension as the schools of North Belfast closed. It was not unusual to see army vehicles parked down the middle of the Crumlin Road to safeguard the pupils of different schools as they made their way home.

Little did I think that, in thirty years time, I would see police and army once again deal with children going to and from school.

When the need arose, I was invited to celebrate Mass for detainees in Long Kesh. This was a whole new world to me as I was photographed by the army on arrival and relieved of all my possessions. Then there were two hours in the compound to be spent celebrating Confession, Mass or whatever the men there wished me to do. Never did I find anything but unfailing courtesy and welcome.

One little service I could offer was to carry out phone numbers of wives, girlfriends, family and friends to be phoned with greetings from a loved one. Many Sunday nights were spent on the phone, talking to people whom I would never see but who appreciated the contact.

It was during these years living in Crossgar that I learned how much fun the local children derived from my Wicklow accent. For example, dropping of the letter 'h' made the time of Sunday afternoon devotions 'tree tirty' instead of three-thirty.

Having a Republic of Ireland driving licence proved a major obstacle at the many military and police road checks that cropped up frequently. There was no photograph on it and a lot of it looked to be in a 'foreign' language. Eventually, I did a driving test in Downpatrick. The day of the test was so foggy that after a few minutes, I was instructed to return to the test centre. On arrival, I was given the news that I had passed!

Over the years, I kept contact with many of the friends made in the early 1970s. I felt enormous sadness when I was transferred from Crossgar back to Dublin in 1974. After starting with a lot of fear, I had come to love my life as a priest during those years. The schools visited, the weekend Masses in Downpatrick and surrounding parishes – all had become part of a life I loved. People were so kind and so appreciative.

I came from Bray, where Catholic, Protestant and people of no religion lived and worked without tension, but I had gone to the Christian Brothers primary school in Greystones, where my mother was born. She told stories of Greystones being called 'Little Belfast' as a strong Protestant influence was apparent there as she grew up. Her wish was that my brother and sister and I would grow up to respect and appreciate people, without distinction.

From 1974 until 1986 I was in the Passionist community in Mount Argus, Dublin. I preached parish missions and other retreats. At 34 years of age, I was elected by my fellow Passionists as their Provincial Superior and served as best I could for six years. It was during this time that I came to know something of Africa, where fellow priests and brothers minister in Botswana and South Africa.

In many ways once Africa's red clay and dust gets into your blood they never leave you. I remember standing in Soweto and feeling sad that so many people had to live there because of the colour of their skin. I will never forget that experience. When years later, during the Holy Cross protest, I was to meet Archbishop Desmond Tutu I knew I was meeting a 'giant' of our times.

From a church aspect, I was sad to know that the iniquity of apartheid was underpinned by a reading of the scriptures that saw it as God's plan and will. The Dutch Reformed Church was one of the mainstays of the apartheid system. However, other Christian churches and their clergy were among the most vocal opponents of the iniquitous apartheid regime. When religion can support injustice directed against a people on the basis of the colour of their skin it becomes dangerous. The role of churches in Ireland can be seen to have certain parallels with what I saw in South Africa.

When my term as Provincial Superior ended in the mid-1980s, I was given an opportunity to take a break and return to study. For two years, I lived and studied in San Francisco, USA. Living in a city parish gave me daily contact with the people of that great and interesting city. In the San Francisco church grounds there was a parish school. It was one of my duties to celebrate Mass for the children once a month. They came from all over the world and fewer than 50 per cent were Catholic. The nuns trained all – of whatever religion or none – to come to Mass.

Life there was so interesting and challenging. It was being gradually realised that AIDS was of epidemic proportions. The local press in San Francisco would regularly publish lists of people, both well-known and not, who had died in the previous month from this killer disease.

The cook at the church where I lived announced one day to the assembled priests that he had been diagnosed as having the disease. None of us knew what to do and neither did he. Eventually, a lovely lady who cleaned in our house – a grandmother – asked him what she could do for him. His answer will always remain with me: 'Just hold me and hug me.' The feeling of being a 'leper' was the worst part of his suffering, he explained. I was one who had caused that pain without realising it. A simple hug was all he craved.

While studying at the University of San Francisco, I volunteered to train as a school counsellor in a poor area of the city. Once a week, I would go there to see whatever children were referred to me. Most of them were of Central American origin and often their parents and grandparents had little English.

Part of our training to do this work was to become familiar with the issue of child sexual abuse and child neglect. There was strict Californian state law that required allegations of child sex abuse to be reported. The forms for this reporting had to be carried whenever children were being seen. Not to report such allegations to the authorities would lead to the teacher or counsellor being questioned by the police. The wisdom of this approach as early as the 1980s in California is interesting. Through training and supervision volunteer counsellors were in great demand by teachers and parent groups for workshops on this topic.

The decision to return from San Francisco to Dublin was one of the hardest I have made. When I came back to Ireland at the beginning of 1989, I was surprised at the lack of interest or structures to deal with the issues of abuse and neglect. I remember one parish priest being furious when I suggested that I would mention these matters as part of the parish mission. He assured me that such things did not happen in Ireland, whatever about America!

Arriving back at the beginning of 1989, I became involved again in preaching missions and retreats. By this stage school retreat teams of lay people and Passionists were working well. We travelled all over the country and also in England. The female members of these teams contributed so much to our understanding of children and young people.

In 1994 I was elected to the General Government of the Passionists. This meant moving to Rome where the headquarters of the Passionists are situated. Today, the Passionists work in sixty countries around the world and number about 2,500 members. It was my privilege to see the church in action in various parts of the world.

One great advantage was in seeing that there were many ways to be a Catholic and a good human being. While immensely proud of being Irish and grateful for the faith I inherited, I am still surprised at how the Irish way is seen as being the only way to be a believer.

Once again, I had regular opportunities to visit Africa and to see a changed South Africa enjoying freedom and a drive for equality and rights. Sadly I also saw something of the war and pain in the Democratic Republic of Congo (formerly Zaire).

Most striking was that as vocations dropped in much of Europe, North America, Canada, Australia and other countries of the 'first world', there was to be seen a blossoming of vocations in Africa and many parts of the southern hemisphere. Often whole seminaries and religious houses had to turn down applicants because of lack of space and finances. There is a message for the church here and one that has received a lot of comment and analysis in recent years.

A long visit to Indonesia brought me into contact with the people of Asia. It was almost too much to take in. The tsunami of 26 December 2004 decimated parts of Indonesia that I had visited – it is heartbreaking to think that so many beautiful children and adults met such a cruel and unexpected death.

I loved my life there as living in Rome was no penance. Close observation of the Vatican helped me to see some pluses and many minuses. To live in the city of Peter and Paul and of so many who have lived and died for Christ is special, and their presence there almost tangible. The Coliseum, Pantheon, Forum and other sites remind you that you are in a living museum.

It was my privilege to meet with the late Pope John Paul II on a number of occasions. The first time was in 1982 while accompanying an African bishop on a visit to the Pope. I was sitting outside when an official brought me to a door which I fully expected to find led out into the street. Instead, it was the door of the Pope's private study.

There stood the Pope and I was not able to utter a word! He looked on me with sympathy and simply took my hands in his and said, 'Hello'. Then he invited me in for a chat and enquired about family members in Ireland and sent each one a rosary beads as a gift.

While in Rome from 1994 onwards, I met Pope John Paul on a number of occasions but nothing could equal that first unexpected encounter. Once, when attending an ordination of a Passionist student in Germany in the mid-1990s, I met Cardinal Ratzinger and concelebrated Mass with him in a small Bavarian chapel the next morning. Over breakfast, he asked about Ireland and in particular the situation in the North.

There is a danger of believing that the Vatican is the Catholic Church. To see so many priests and religious occupied in offices while the world cries out for priests, nurses and teachers for God's people is hard to understand. This can so easily breed a clericalism that kills the Spirit. It is difficult to speak of a shortage of vocations when so many priests are seen to staff offices and work in administration – jobs that could be done by lay people. Also the closed culture of the Vatican encourages a sense that keeping things as they are is a priority. Urgent matters such as a married clergy or the ordination of women are excluded from the agenda.

What a liberation it would be if every parish throughout the world were asked to spend time in prayer to see what the Holy Spirit is asking today and for tomorrow. But even to suggest this is considered by some to be a mark of disloyalty.

When my Rome assignment finished in 2000 I was given an extra year in Italy so that I might return to university to study. I spent a wonderful year at the Angelicum University in Rome studying for a licence to teach theology. Not that I believe I have a vocation to be a seminary teacher!

In November 2000 I received a phone call from my superior in Dublin, Fr Martin Coffey. He asked if I was sitting down. I had been expecting this call and thought I might be asked to accept an assignment back in Dublin.

He asked me to go Holy Cross, Belfast. I was dumbfounded. In spite of my previous contacts with Belfast, I could think of so many others better qualified and suitable for this assignment. When there was no sound from my side of the call, he asked if I was still there. It was not that I was opposed to this move, more that I was surprised.

When I asked him if people in Ardoyne had asked for me to be sent as their parish priest, he answered no. When I asked him if the Passionist community of Holy Cross had asked for me as their superior, he answered no. Then I asked him why he was asking me to go there. Truthfully he replied that he had no rational answer to that question.

I asked him for 24 hours to think the matter over. Next day, I accepted the assignment which was due to begin in summer 2001. Over the thirty years I had spent as a priest, I had never asked to go to a particular place and I had never refused an assignment. Overall, I had been happy. On that basis I accepted but I asked for one consideration. By that stage, Fr Martin was so relieved that I had accepted that he was ready to listen to my request.

My one request was that I have as little as possible to do with the schools of the parish. I did this not because I don't see them as our future, but because of my lack of knowledge of Boards of Governors, interviewing for teachers, budgets and the like. He readily agreed, adding that I would have practically nothing to do with schools in Ardoyne. I believe that God has a sense of humour! My plans were not His.

With that matter settled, I got back to my studies. Christmas came and went and the prospect of completing a thesis and taking final exams in June 2001 loomed large. It was good to be a student again.

Every morning in Rome, I checked the internet to see what the news was overnight. On the morning of 20 June 2001, I saw that there had been trouble the previous day on Ardoyne Road near to Holy Cross Girls' School. There was not much detail. My reaction was relief that no one was reported as having been hurt. My other feeling was that this would be long over before I got there in late July.

Little did I know that this would become part of the lives of so many people, including myself. During those lovely days in Rome, I sometimes wondered about what lay ahead. I had my dreams and I had my fears. With so much time to read and reflect, I was very happy with the lack of pressure and the absence of the long air journeys of the previous six years.

Had I known what lay ahead in the next few years, I might have seen that God was perhaps preparing me for something I could never have imagined in my wildest dreams.

Truthfully, I looked forward to going to Holy Cross as the beginning of my winding down towards retirement. This was my opportunity to work full-time in a parish. One of the members of the community of Holy Cross came for a weekend to Rome and suggested how I might plan the parish work for the coming three years. His experience was admittedly great because he had served there for many years. However, the views of the people were the starting point as far as I was concerned rather than a plan devised in the monastery.

During the years preaching missions and retreats, I had come to admire some wonderful parishes served by great priests, laity and religious. I was immensely saddened by the lifeless parishes I saw where people's views were excluded and so much hurt caused.

The long-awaited examinations came and went and were not as bad as I had feared. Then I had the sad task of packing up after seven very happy years in Rome. I had to choose what to bring back and what to discard. Boxes were packed, goodbyes said to many good friends at places like the Irish College, the Irish embassies that had been so welcoming, the Irish houses of religious orders and even a few of the local Irish pubs who had welcomed me to watch Irish sports events.

Then there was a final journey along the familiar route to Leonardo da Vinci Airport, Rome – a route that over the previous seven years I had travelled so often. One part of me was heartbroken and another part was looking forward to a new challenge and new opportunities. It was with enthusiasm and optimism that I landed at Dublin Airport in July 2001.

Deliberately I had not made contact with Holy Cross from the time of my being asked to go there, but obviously I had read accounts of what was happening. Fr Kenneth Brady and Fr Gary Donegan were the superiors there. The full reality came home to me when I met with Fr Gary on 17 July in Dublin to hear from him about what were the main issues awaiting us as the new administration at Holy Cross.

He brought with him a list of items. Naturally, there were items relating to community and parish matters at Holy Cross. But central was the situation at Holy Cross Girls' School. He was deeply concerned about the situation and advised me of its seriousness. He told me many sad stories of the violence associated with 12 July marches and the nights following. He painted a grim but accurate story of nightly rioting and hurt.

I was heartbroken to think about such a breakdown of living among people at this time of ceasefire and political agreement. Gary left me with much to think about as he went back to Belfast to do what he could in that situation.

After he had gone, I sat there for a while wondering if it would not be better to take a plane back to Rome! It was a daunting challenge that faced all those who were involved in what was happening.

I told Gary that I would be in Belfast around teatime on 27 July. It was a Friday afternoon. On arrival at Central Station, Belfast, I was met by Fr Myles Kavanagh, a member of the parish team in Holy Cross. I asked him how things were. He shook his head and said little.

Fr Kenneth would remain parish priest for another few days after my arrival. A warm letter of welcome to the Diocese of Down and Connor, from Bishop Patrick Walsh, awaited me. I set about finding my way around the monastery and discovering where everything was kept.

Sleep was not as easy as it had been in Rome with the sound of rioting at the back of the monastery the night I arrived. On Sunday, 29 July, I offered the 11 a.m. and 12.30 p.m. Masses and people could see this new person who had arrived from Rome. For my part, I didn't know what to think. I knew that I would need to meet a lot of people and listen more than speak.

The following day, I met with Anne Tanney, Principal of Holy Cross Girls' School. I had known Anne and her husband, Pat, since the early 1970s when I used to visit Holy Cross. Anne had been a teacher at Holy Cross in its days in Chief Street, Ardoyne, before it was burned. Then the school moved to its present site on Ardoyne Road. It opened its doors for pupils on 12 May 1969. The school was built in the grounds of the old Wheatfield Seminary, previously owned by the Passionists. Anne was to go on to become principal and retired only in summer 2004. The Mission Statement of the school is interesting:

In Holy Cross Girls' we aim to provide a happy, secure, challenging, learning environment in which the child can grow into a self-confident, educated, resourceful, faith-inspired young person; provide an environment where parents feel welcome and empowered to help in their children's education.

At this meeting, I confided in Anne my wish to have little to do with the schools if this was at all possible. I could see the surprise on her face and so I didn't pursue the matter. I heard from her something of what had happened on 19 June and during the weeks before the end of term.

There was no easy solution, she assured me, and I believed her. It was essential that the Board of Governors meet to elect a new chair following the departure of Fr Kenneth as parish priest. I indicated to Anne that I would be asking the Board to select someone other than me for this important post. A meeting was set for the following Monday, 6 August, Feast of the Transfiguration.

Meanwhile, the welcome from parishioners was warm and genuine. People stopped me in the street to ask if I was their new priest and assured me of their prayers and support. People with particular concerns came to see me about the serious situation. Everyone who spoke to me about Holy Cross Girls' School emphasised the seriousness of the situation and the danger we would face in just four weeks' time. Their comments brought me face to face with the reality of what was happening.

On Wednesday, 1 August, I had my first formal meeting with the Passionist Community. Looking back on what I said that day, I think I got some things right and some wrong. I got right that our strength lay in our being a faith community based on companionship, Eucharist and prayer. I also suggested that after the achievements of successive communities at Holy Cross since 1869, and more particularly over the past thirty years, we should establish a 'media desk' to spread the message of the Cross as it unfolds before us. In this age of internet and electronic media I had learned from living outside Ireland how valuable those media are. I wanted to see us commenting not solely on news items but on matters of pastoral practice and spirituality.

This got a mixed reception. One member of the community suggested that if we were to make comments in public, we could be burned out of the monastery. I thought this a little extreme but it came true even before any media statement could be made.

Fr Gary had kindly arranged a meal of welcome for me at a nearby hotel that very night. It was a lovely gesture and six of us sat down together to a meal. Two of our number, due to age or illness could not join us. Fr Brendan, our senior member, was then almost 90 years of age, the other Br Paschal has been a member of Holy Cross community for over fifty years. We assured them that we would not be late home.

On returning to Holy Cross at about 10.30 p.m., we were met by police in boiler suits. A door in the back wall of the monastery on the Woodvale Road had been broken down. A flammable liquid had been poured though a window into a storeroom at the back of the kitchen and set alight. The items stored there took flame and it was only a matter of time until the building would have been alight. Fortunately, a passing army patrol spotted the flames and tackled the blaze until the fire service arrived.

The two elderly occupants of the monastery were blissfully unaware of the drama, but it could have been a very serious incident. I remarked to my colleague who had counselled against speaking to the media that arson attacks could happen even while we remained silent.

The following day, I was asked by Downtown Radio to comment on the fire. That was the first media interview I gave in my life and I was very nervous.

My only other experience of any form of media had been making a video on the life of St Paul of the Cross, founder of the Passionists, while living in Italy. The budget was extremely limited and I was asked to drive the film crew while shooting the video. The 'star' was Martin Sheen, latterly of *West Wing* fame on TV, and he proved to be a delight to meet and work with. Eventually, I was asked to take a small part in the production. It is a huge honour to have worked with Martin Sheen!

On the Friday of my first full week at Holy Cross I was to visit the sick in one area of the parish. They told me that it would take a long time for me to match the standard of Fr Kenneth who had been with them for many years – I knew I was on trial and a verdict would eventually be given.

The strength of a parish lies in its people. A priest can help bring out the best in them. He can also contribute to killing the workings of the Spirit among the people. As my first week came to an end I was struck by the depth of people's faith and could only imagine how hope had stayed alive over the previous 132 years of Holy Cross.

Already I knew that whatever we were being called to at this time would be based on the work of those who had gone before. The sheer goodness and dedication of generations of people creates a tradition that is almost tangible.

One of the personal truths that I could never escape during the previous thirty years as a priest was my own sinfulness. To present myself as somehow perfect, besides being untrue, is an obstacle to growth.

In the same way, no parish is without its divisions and sinfulness. Soon I would discover that Holy Cross was not only divided from its Protestant neighbours but divisions within were just as real. These too would affect the events that were about to unfold.

My first week at Holy Cross came to an end and I had, at least, survived it. But I felt that more was yet to happen. It would not be long until I realised just how much more.

CHAPTER TWO

OVER THAT FIRST weekend one item was foremost in my mind – the Board of Governors meeting scheduled for 6 August at 7 p.m. in Holy Cross Monastery. Anne Tanney was the only member I knew, and I was both looking forward to it and dreading it. It was my hope that progress would be made to resolve the enormous problems that had dominated everything since my arrival a few days previously.

In those few days I had a 'crash course' in educational matters. The Catholic Council for Maintained Schools (CCMS) deals with Catholic education and takes care of the Trustees' concerns. Belfast Education and Library Board (BELB) deals with buildings and maintenance, as well as some internal matters. The Department of Education of Northern Ireland (DENI) is the government body dealing with education at all levels.

The governors of a school have responsibility for its education, health and safety, budget and all policies. Governors are a voluntary group and give of their time and effort out of love and concern for the children, teachers and staff of the school. No praise of mine for these people who serve as governors could do justice to the contribution they make.

On the Holy Cross Board of Governors there are representatives of trustees, DENI, BELB, parents and teachers. The key people in the leadership of any school are the teachers, staff and parents. Of these the principal is crucial. In Holy Cross where the one Board of

Governors served both schools we were blessed in having Anne Tanney in the girls' school and Terry Laverty in the boys' school. Both turned out to be towers of strength.

One great loss at this time was that the teacher representative had retired and had not been replaced. Also, there was no parent-teacher group. Such a group could have made a great difference.

Each of the governors gave me a great welcome. I could see the sorrow in their eyes as they looked at this innocent man from abroad about to join them. The meeting began with a prayer and introductions. Warm tributes were paid to the retiring chairperson, Fr Kenneth Brady. The events of June had disrupted a more formal farewell and thanks.

The first item on the agenda was the election of the chairperson. I immediately asked that I should not be considered for this position as I had just arrived and had little knowledge of the education system. Genuinely I was aware that all the others present were better qualified for this post. During a short discussion, I was asked to reconsider my position. It was pointed out to me that nobody could know what September would bring and what might be asked of the chairperson. Solely because of this request my name went forward and, as the minutes record, 'this was unanimously agreed and passed'.

This was something I had not expected. It was an enormous act of trust in me by such an experienced group. I was just one week there, and still I was trusted with this leadership.

The Glenbryn residents' prevention of children from going to school along the only accepted route of Ardoyne Road is recorded in the minutes of this first meeting I attended. Even at this early stage, I was completely unhappy that this should have happened and determined that it should not be repeated. Not having been there from 19 June until the end of the school term, I could not make any informed comment.

When I read the headlines of the Irish newspapers of 20 June in my room in Rome, I had noticed that there had been disturbances at Holy Cross Girls' Primary School the previous afternoon. It made for sad reading. It was my hope and prayer that a solution would be found to allow the children to continue going to school without hindrance.

Unfortunately, the subsequent days brought further accounts of protest on Ardoyne Road near to the school.

Being an optimist as well as being filled with hope, I was sure that the matter would be resolved before I arrived there later that summer. It was difficult to find out what had brought such a sudden and serious eruption of trouble as was being reported.

The *Guardian* newspaper carries an interesting account of what took place on 19 June 2001. The newspaper quotes one loyalist woman who says she saw the incident on Ardoyne Road that day. Her opinion of the account that a car going to Holy Cross School drove at those on a ladder putting up flags, was 'It's lies, they didn't drive at the ladder.' This named lady from Glenbryn says that the parents began arriving at around 2 p.m. to collect their children from Holy Cross School. A car drove up Ardoyne Road, she says, and those putting up the flags threw the ladder at the back window of the car. It screeched to a halt, the men got out, and instantly there was fighting and 'all hell broke loose'.

According to the newspaper account, this lady spoke to the RUC officers when they arrived on Ardoyne Road. She told them that she was a witness to what had happened. She claims that she was ignored and never asked to give her version of what took place.

One of the simplest accounts of the events of that day was written for me by an 11-year-old pupil of the school caught up in those events. She calls it '19th June'.

> When the protestors blocked off the Ardoyne Road they were shouting, yelling and throwing stones. When I saw the policemen that blocked the road and would not let us up we were upset. I was crying my eyes out and was taking it bad. When I was in the school I could walk up normally until I was in P.7. When I was in P.5 to P.7 the women and men gived [sic] us biscuits and I don't know why they turned against us. I was unhappy because I never got to do my leavers play or Mass. We never got to do sports day either. I never got to say a proper goodbye to the teachers. Now I'm glad I'm in secondary school so I don't have to go through it again as I know it's worse for the girls. I hope it would end and hope the protestors would wise up to themselves.

The governors had decided to move the sports day, mentioned above, to the grounds of St Gabriel's College, for Wednesday, 27 June 2001.

Something of the seriousness of the situation can be gleaned from the fact that the Irish National Teachers' Organisation saw 'this direction to be unreasonable in light of the prevailing extenuating circumstances in the area, which are prejudicial to the health, safety and welfare of the teachers and pupils.' The INTO 'advised its members not to participate in these activities in St Gabriel's School'. (letter to Board of Governors, 25 June 2001).

Eventually the sports day was not held and we can see something of the sadness of one little girl recounted above. She gives us a great insight into the mind of a child who experienced the first few days of this protest.

To this day (2005), teachers, parents and therapists are attempting to assess the effects of the events of the protest and subsequent sporadic attacks on the school since. It is far too early to give any definite assessment and only time will tell what are the long-term consequences.

Much the same can be said of the children in Glenbryn who were brought to the protest and must have been deeply affected by what they saw and heard. It is my hope that these children will be helped and will recover well.

It is lovely to think of a time when Holy Cross children got biscuits from the local residents as they made their way to or from school. With so much violence in this area over the previous thirty years it was a source of great pride that by and large schools were regarded as off limits for attacks. This is borne out in observations made by the Lawyers Alliance for Justice in Ireland:

Even though most Catholics had been likewise expelled from their homes in Glenbryn, Holy Cross pupils and their parents walked for years in relative peace along the sidewalks of the Protestant enclave. In fact, many of the mothers escorting their daughters to school under protest in 2001 had safely taken the same route to school when they were children. Not until June of 2001, when Glenbryn residents decided to block all Catholic passage along

Ardoyne Road, was there any reason for the Holy Cross pupils to fear their daily walk to school.

(*Report on Holy Cross Girls' Primary School,* September 2001)

An important fact to remember is that the children of Holy Cross and Wheatfield Primary School, the state school opposite, shared bus trips and projects. The teachers of both schools worked closely together and knew each other. This is also part of the history of the protest. The trips of 2000-2001 planned between Holy Cross and Wheatfield Primary Schools had been meticulously planned and had been a great success.

Teachers from both schools had co-operated with each other for the sake of the children. Parents had heard the stories brought home from the trips taken together. They would have heard the names of children from the 'other' school. Because this was the way the two schools worked and respected each other, this form of co-operation was taken for granted.

When the breakdown took place at an adult level it was the children and the schools who suffered most. Later, the way forward in education will be addressed. Suffice to say here that in examining integrated education we should question whether we are asking children and schools to integrate in a divided society. The values and courage of those involved in integrated schools deserve our admiration. It is therefore necessary not to ask schools to carry a burden of responsibility if the surrounding community does not work for the same values.

The programme of co-operation for the year before the outbreak of the protest makes interesting if sad reading:

ClassVenue	Venue
Reception	1. Ballysillan Leisure Centre
	2. Belfast Castle
	3. Chicken Run at Wheatfield
Primary One	1. Ice Breaker games at H.C.
	2. Visit from Zoo at Wheatfield
Primary Two	1. Ulster Folk Park, Cultra
	2. Chicken Run at Wheatfield
	3. Art Day at Wheatfield

Primary Three	1. Mount Stewart
	2. The Linen Centre, Lisburn
	3. Art Day at Wheatfield
Primary Four	1. Down Museum
	2. Crossgar Wildlife Centre
	3. Tayto Factory
	4. Art Day at Wheatfield
Primary Five	1. Ulster Museum
	2. Navan Centre, Armagh
	3. Poetry/Dance Day at H.C.
Primary Six	1. Peatlands Park
	2. Down Museum
Primary Seven	1. Castleward
	2. Ulster American Folk Park

What a tragedy that such wonderful and rich co-operation could be wiped out by events that unfolded. Years of work were destroyed in a few minutes, and it is taking years to get back even to a beginning of such wonderful and healthy co-operation.

There are numerous examples around the world where people have gone through the struggle to dismantle hatred and suspicion and build trust and confidence in each other. Often from a distance, people wonder why it is taking so long and many lose interest and hope. Some question whether there will ever be peace in such places.

In 1978, when in South Africa for the first time to spend time with Passionists there, I was struck by how people held on to the inherited stereotypes. It seemed that because of the apartheid system, they seldom got to know someone of a different race or culture. A place like Soweto stood as a sad monument to the theory of separate development.

Not only in South Africa, but in Ireland also, stereotyping is alive and well. The problem is that we cannot reason our way out of stereotypes because people don't reason their way into them. Even though much went on in both Holy Cross and Wheatfield Primary Schools to break down these attitudes, it is often what adults say that reinforces these stereotypes in the minds of young people.

Child should never be set against child and there must have been bewilderment in the eyes of the children going to school as they spotted a friend of better days. A little girl walking to school would say to me, 'Look there is ...' and point out someone they knew among the protestors. This was extremely painful for them.

Most likely some of the little girls brought to the protest must have wondered why their friends of yesterday were now no longer so.

In an address at Mass in Holy Cross on Sunday, 24 June 2001, Bishop Patrick Walsh spoke of 'an ugly week'. He went on to say that 'what took place was unpardonable and groups or individuals responsible for fomenting the expressions of hatred and sectarianism which so blighted this area have much to answer for.' He spoke of the events of previous days as 'something totally reprehensible in preventing young children attending school. That such young children were exposed to such terrifying experiences must be condemned by all right-minded people.'

Little could he or those listening to him at Mass that day know that far worse was to follow. It must have been hard to imagine at that stage that things could get worse for girls aged four to eleven years. But events unimaginable at that time were to occur after the summer holidays.

A factor seldom highlighted came to light in the minutes of the 6 August Board of Governors meeting. A representative of CCMS told us that 'three years previously' there had been 'an ongoing interface issue'. A proposal had been made to erect a wall on the Ardoyne Road between the two communities but eventually the matter was dropped. He advised 'that the current issue seemed to be a continuation of the situation.' It is of great credit to all concerned that this matter was resolved at the time. The education and safety of the children was the prime concern, and the school went on to have a number of years of peace and good education before the events of 19 June 2001.

On 22 June 2001, CCMS had made a statement that:

All children have a right to be educated in an atmosphere free from fear and disturbance. As a society we must respect that right to education for that is the key not only to the future of our children but indeed the community as a whole and any actions that effectively denies children what is a basic Human Right should be condemned. (CCMS Press Release, 22 June 2001)

The wish of Glenbryn residents to have a wall across or adjacent to Ardoyne Road would surface again as the protest developed. There was already a 'peace wall' running between Glenbryn and Alliance Avenue.

Even at this early stage, it was clearly accepted 'that there are a number of community issues that need to be resolved.' From the beginning this was and continued to be the position of the governors.

The people of Glenbryn had issues that were real to them and therefore had to be taken seriously by us as neighbours and as a Board of Governors. It does not help to say that these issues are not real or well founded. If I am afraid, even if I have no reason to be so, your telling me that my fear is groundless does not solve anything. To this day, I believe that the issues of our neighbours in Glenbryn must be taken seriously, and as presented. Without this starting position, dialogue and resolution are not possible.

As I sat at my first meeting of the governors I learned something that I will carry with me to the grave. The only thing that could have prevented the awful events that were to follow was the acceptance that you cannot stop children from going to school.

No matter how it is dressed up, it is 'totally reprehensible', in the words of Bishop Walsh on 24 June. To get the children back to school safely and without danger was the only issue that would occupy me. All other issues, including those of the protestors, would be dealt with only when this prime and central issue was resolved.

At a meeting following the disturbances of 19 June a committee comprising community leaders had been set up to deal with the issue of the children going to school free from danger. A parents' group had also been set up to deal with the school issue. It was made up of four individual parents of pupils attending the school and was known as the Right to Education group (RTE).

Both groups had the same sole aim – the safe return of the children to school. Nobody could doubt the urgency felt by parents to address this most awful situation. It was not that they didn't know about other community issues in Glenbryn but their children were their priority.

On Tuesday, 26 June 2001 the RTE clarified its aim and function. Proposals had been put to the committee by the residents of Glenbryn. It was made clear that these proposals were not rejected, but the RTE had some difficulties with some of them. Those on the committee were keen to point out that they were not political representatives, but parents whose sole concern was their children's right to safe passage to their school.

Rightly, the parents separated the school issue from these other important matters. Anne Tanney expressed her concern that the Right to Education group did not include any representatives from the governors, to give a school perspective on the issue. This was important for me to hear. It seemed that the governors were seen as marginal by some.

It was proposed that an offer be made to the parents' group to augment its numbers with two representatives from the governors. This seemed crucial and the proposal was adopted and arrangements made for an approach to be made to implement this. Two of the governors were nominated.

However, by 8 August it was clear that the offer by the governors to join with the parents' group had been rejected. The reason for the rejection was that negotiations with the parents' counterparts in the Glenbryn community were focused and that there seemed to be a possibility that the situation would be resolved quite quickly. The RTE also felt that that the addition of two Board members could alter the representational balance in meetings between the groups.

The parents' group agreed to reconsider the offer of the Board if the current negotiations failed to resolve the situation. By 11 August, it emerged that a resolution seemed far away.

This news saddened me greatly. While understanding the RTE's reasons for not accepting two governors, I was looking for a way to bring together all who were working for the same purpose – namely, the safe return to the school of the children. In discussions with Rev Stewart Heaney of the Church of Ireland and Rev Norman Hamilton of the Presbyterian Church, I became more aware of wider community issues which needed urgent attention once the children were safely back at school.

Later, I learned that a skilled mediation group was also working with the parents and the protestors to seek a resolution. This was to be welcomed as any and every effort had to be made to ensure that the children could return to school in peace on 3 September. This was only weeks away.

It struck me as unsatisfactory that there was little contact between the governors and the mediation group. There was no doubting the group's professional work and good intentions. But ultimately the decision to reopen the school in September could be taken only by the governors in dialogue with the parents.

By mid-August, the mediation group had organised a series of meetings involving the Ardoyne Focus Group, parents (Right to Education committee) and Concerned Residents of Upper Ardoyne (CRUA). There was no invitation to the governors to become involved despite their statutory obligation to ensure the safe return of the children to school.

It is not surprising that at the 6 August meeting, I was quite concerned at the role of the school governors in resolving the dispute. In my own estimation contact would have to be made with parents and anyone in the community who could help.

Shortly after 6 August, I was invited to attend a meeting in the Focus Group offices at the top of Brompton Park, Ardoyne. This community group works on a wide range of issues within the community. When I mentioned that I would like to attend this meeting, I was told that it was not advisable for me to be seen in the Focus Group premises. It began to dawn on me that divisions within Ardoyne also existed. Much later, I was to learn something of the depth of these.

As the new parish priest, I was still unknown by sight to most in the community, and I was delighted with the opportunity to make contact with some members of the Right to Education committee.

With just over three weeks to go before school restarted I was beginning to feel that greater efforts would need to be made. The efforts being made have been described as sporadic and it was suggested that more could and might have been done to resolve the conflict before autumn. This does not do justice to efforts that were made not only by parents and school authorities but also by concerned people connected to the Glenbryn community.

Shortly after my arrival in Holy Cross, the Rev. Stewart Heaney, Rector Church of Ireland Ballysillan, invited me to join him and his family for a meal in their home. Stewart and Fr Kenneth had done so much for community relations and church co-operation, and it was a most enjoyable evening that we spent together. This gesture of his will always remain with me as a treasured memory. Later, through a misunderstanding our relationship as pastors in the same area ran into difficulties. But his and his family's kindness and welcome far outweigh any subsequent difficulties.

Another contact made in August 2001 was to last right up to the present. Rev Norman Hamilton, Presbyterian Church Ballysillan, called to see me to share his view of what was happening in our community. He was deeply affected by the depth of the divisions and concerned about what lay ahead as the reopening of the school drew ever closer. Norman and his family offered a welcome to me that meant a great deal.

Ministers of other churches in the area were also most welcoming. To this day, many are in regular contact and have proved helpful and supportive. Even at the worst moments of the protest, these good people did not lose their nerve or walk away. The sad part was that much of this type of contact had to be kept at a discreet level.

Making these contacts brought home to me how sad the divisions between our churches are. The many great efforts over the years to bring about the unity of Christians and the dialogue between religions are to be applauded. In the context in which I now found myself, the division among Christians had taken on a life-and-death dimension.

While it might not be possible to bring about Christian unity or conclude a satisfactory agreement among world religions, events locally and internationally impose an urgency that is often lacking.

Every moment of the day and often late into the night people were working to find a resolution. Prayer was offered insistently and frequently for this intention and I was enormously encouraged by phone calls and messages from people of goodwill who prayed for a safe return to school for the children.

A kind person greatly concerned for the children spoke to Fr Gary and said that a Miraculous Medal for each child would offer protection. A week later, I was contacted by the Royal Mail to say that a brown envelope addressed to me had been found to contain metal. When the 'suspect' package had been dealt with by explosive experts there remained only the melted-down remains of over two hundred medals! The intention of the person was good.

The governors met again on 13 August to see what could be done. Through CCMS contacts with the Department of Education it emerged that the First Minister Designate, Sir Reg Empey, and the Deputy First Minister, Mr Seamus Mallon, had offered their assistance to resolve the issue. While this was greatly appreciated, the proximity of the return to school did not allow for briefings and meetings.

Contact had also been made by the American Consul based in Belfast, Barbara Stevenson, who became a valued friend and a source of great encouragement until her return to the United States in 2004.

The governors' meeting of 13 August went on late into the night as we searched for a way forward that would guarantee the safety of the children and afterwards open up a way to address the issues raised by the Glenbryn community. A strategy was agreed:

1. A subcommittee – made up of the two school principals, CCMS representative and me – was to meet the community group made up substantially of parents, to obtain a clear and full understanding of progress to date. This was to take place the following Monday ahead of the Board meeting that evening.

2. The subcommittee was to advise this group of the governors' intention to have a meeting with the parents of the pupils of the school and to invite the group to participate.

3. This meeting with all the parents was arranged to take place in Holy Cross Boys' School canteen on Thursday, 23 August, at 7.30 p.m. A letter inviting parents to this meeting was to be sent out on Monday, 20 August by Anne Tanney.

4. The CCMS representative would report back regarding the offer of assistance by the First and Deputy First Minister.

By now it was clear that the police would also have to become involved in the preparations for the return to school. It was going to be delicate as there are issues around policing that still persist. Being a newcomer, and in many ways an outsider, was an advantage. The determining factor was the safety of the children and their parents as the return to school drew ever closer.

Assistant Chief Constable Alan McQuillan and Area Commander Roger Maxwell came to see me on various occasions. The starting point was that Chief Constable Ronnie Flanagan had given an assurance that the children could return to school by the Ardoyne Road in September. With that assurance, I set about meeting with as many parents as I could.

The Feast of the Assumption, 15 August, was imminent and an invitation was extended to all families to attend the Vigil Mass on 14 August. This gave me an opportunity to speak about the return to school, ahead of the 23 August meeting of parents asked for by the school governors. The homily I delivered that night spoke to parents of their great gift from God of being co-creators with Him. They were reminded that the children they had brought into this world are the most precious gift that God can give a person. I pointed out that the Church teaches that the right and duty of parents to educate their children is primordial and inalienable and that this right and duty to educate their child does not come from the church, government or any other source. It is their right from God and nobody can take it from them or interfere with it. It is clearly set out in the teaching of the Church that parents have the right to choose for their child a school that corresponds to their own convictions. This right is fundamental and public authorities have the duty of guaranteeing this parental right and of ensuring the practical conditions for its existence.

It seemed to me important to go back to basics and let these good parents – now so troubled – know that they were in charge. Nobody had a right to challenge their guardianship and care of their children and their education. Social and community issues are real and need addressing, but the inalienable right of the parents regarding the education of their children needed to be clearly spelled out and guaranteed.

That night, I gave an assurance that the parish of Holy Cross would ensure that all the schools of the parish would be open to receive children sent there by parents:

Let there be no confusion. The education of children is not up for debate or negotiation. It is so fundamental a right of the child and the parent that we as a parish and as a religious community will not stop to pray and to work to ensure that indeed the children will return to school in peace and quiet…This is the promise that we as your parish make tonight. (Homily, 14 August 2001)

It is always hard to assess what effect a sermon has on its hearers. That night many parents, meeting me for the first time, seemed relieved that a clear message had been delivered. The meeting the following week would continue our planning for the return to school.

Meeting again on 20 August in Holy Cross Monastery, the governors learned that meetings of the parents' group with the Glenbryn community had still not resolved the issues, although there was a glimmer of hope that a resolution might be found. A tentative meeting to discuss a successful outcome was arranged.

That evening, I got the distinct impression that all the best efforts were not going to succeed. This was not the fault of any person or group but somehow it seemed to me – as one just arrived – that the sidelining of governors in the frenzied days following the outbreak of violence on 19 June was proving costly.

It was now clear to me from discussions with the RUC and at this meeting of school governors that we would have to begin to outline options to put to the parents at our meeting in three days' time.

The conclusions we reached included asking CCMS to make contact with any group or body that might be able to help in resolving the conflict before the children went back to school. It was agreed that I would open and close the parents' meeting and that it would be chaired by Anne Tanney. It was considered important to have an update from the parents' group on its discussions with the Glenbryn community representatives.

On 23 August, the hall of Holy Cross Boys' School was packed by anxious parents seeking to know what was being suggested for the return to school on 3 September. Looking at that attendance, it dawned on me that nobody of any religious or political outlook should have been subjected to such anxiety and worry. If this had been a lobby group or people agitating for some political or social cause, they would have been worthy of support. But to look and see good women and men asking if their children were going to be allowed to return in safety to school was heart-rending. The meeting could have only one focus: 'How do we best ensure that your children return to school in safety and peace?' (address of Aidan Troy, Chair of Board of Governors, 23 August).

I could scarcely believe what I was witnessing. Such a fundamental issue is taken for granted in civilised society. Yet here were we gathered to assess how to get 225 little girls back to school.

The meeting was emotionally charged, which was understandable. Parents showed their single-minded purpose by constantly asking questions about the arrangements for the children getting to school. It was clear to me that the parents would not entertain being told that they could take their children to school by some alternative road and through another school. This had been accepted following the 19 June disturbances, but it was no longer acceptable.

Having listened to all the views the governors asked the parents to come to school as usual on Monday, 3 September. By this stage there was a growing media interest in what was likely to happen.

The work of the parents' committee and the mediation group continued right up to the last minute. There was hope up to the weekend of 1-2 September that some resolution might be found. A final meeting at Belfast Castle ended without a successful outcome.

The governors also continued to work at finding a resolution. I met with parents again on 28 August, and the governors brought forward their meeting to that same night. The other schools in the area were wished a safe return to school.

On 29 August 2001, as the final few days ebbed away, a statement was issued from Holy Cross, making a last appeal to all people of goodwill to ensure a safe and peaceful return to school. It was pointed out that Holy Cross Monastery was ready to help in every way possible. A promise was made to help address contentious issues raised by people in North Belfast and to resolve them. The statement concluded by saying: 'It would be sad and wrong if children were cast in the role of being bargained about. People in both communities are continuing to work and pray for the resolution of this serious situation' (statement re Holy Cross Girls' School, Ardoyne, 29 August 2001).

Prayers were offered at all the weekend Masses that the protest would be called off so that the children could return safely to school and the community issues be examined.

By the end of my first month at Holy Cross, I had spent four weeks meeting a great range of people and learning something of what might lie ahead. Little did I realise how much remained to be learned.

CHAPTER THREE

JUST BEFORE THE return to school, I received a lesson I will never forget. A mother of a pupil offered her support for what the governors were doing to resolve the situation. Her concern was that as I was new to the situation, I was in danger of complicating the sole issue to be dealt with at this critical juncture. She told me never to forget that a family living at point A in Holy Cross Parish wanted to get a child to Holy Cross Girls' School at point B and back home again. Nothing more and nothing less was at stake. She finished by asking a question that still has not been satisfactorily answered: 'Is that too much to ask?' I remembered every day during the protest what that parent had said.

While the previous four weeks in Ardoyne had led me to understand that this was the issue, her clarity stood me in good stead as the morning of 3 September loomed.

On Sunday, 2 September, Fr Gary and I prepared a press release as a final appeal to anyone listening. On an old and slow fax machine, we distributed this appeal to media outlets and any groups or organisations we thought might help. All those in positions of leadership, political or religious, were asked to do everything possible to ensure that the basic freedom to attend school without hindrance be respected. The appeal finished by pointing out that it would be both sad and wrong if children were cast in the role of being bargained about.

In Holy Cross Monastery, there is a small chapel on the top floor that is used daily by the Passionist community. I went there late on the night of 2 September. I went there to pray, but I found that no words would come. I didn't know what to ask God to do. All I could do was to remain there in silence. I had no idea as to what lay ahead, but my hope was that any protest the next morning would be short-lived and low key. I thought of the children who were going to bed excited at the prospect of starting 'big school' the next day. These would be the children who had not been there in June and who would have been spared the awful scenes and violence. I could only imagine something of the expectation as all was prepared for the next morning – those children being just four years of age.

The other classes of the school were also in my prayers and thoughts. In all, 225 little girls, aged four to eleven years of age, were preparing to return to school after the summer holidays. That is all that was happening. All else must be seen in the context of this simple event that would take place all over Ireland, Britain and in countries all over the world. Sometimes people may believe that in some sense there was a demonstration or a march being prepared for on this first weekend of September. It cannot be too strongly stated that children going to school as their parents wished was and remains the core issue on Ardoyne Road in 2001.

The other schools of the area, of all denominations and none, were also in my thoughts and prayers. Education never takes place in a vacuum. The violent summer and the memory of the June disturbances had had their impact on the children of North Belfast. Children hear adults talking and many of the children must have known that Monday, 3 September, would be no ordinary day.

To the best of my knowledge everything possible had been done by so many people to make the return to school as smooth and, in the circumstances, as normal as possible. Parents, mediation workers, the protestors and other individuals and groups had all worked to bring about a final resolution of the dispute that had flared in June. There was always the possibility that events might not be too bad the next day. With that I went to bed.

The day dawned, bright and sunny. Early rising was not a problem for me after seven years living in Rome. Before 6.30 a.m., I was dressed in my black habit, in preparation for 7.30 Mass, and I decided to walk up past Ardoyne shops to Ardoyne Road, at the top of which Holy Cross Girls' School is situated. I wanted to see what preparations had been made.

At this stage, I had no reason to believe that there was any particular danger in doing this. The scene on the road was hard to take in. From detailed discussions with the RUC I had known that the children and their parents had been guaranteed safe passage to school, but I couldn't believe my eyes.

The British Army was in full swing, linking a series of Perspex screens together along the left-hand footpath of Ardoyne Road. There were military and police vehicles everywhere, with personnel shouting instructions to each other. The scene reminded me of a film set for a war movie. The Belfast *News Letter* reported that 400 police officers had been brought in to protect the schoolchildren. The cost of that day's policing was given as £100,000.

It was important to keep reminding myself that the issue was young girls going to school. If that were forgotten, other issues could begin to dominate. This is what eventually happened.

Further up the road, I saw a milk float that could not get past the security-force vehicles. The driver was getting agitated and explained to the police officer that the milk was for Holy Cross School. He was advised to forget about his delivery and go away. That made me wonder what that officer knew.

Because of the activity on the footpath, I was walking on the road. As I got closer to the school, I noticed people coming out of houses and from side streets. I recognised a prominent loyalist politician among them. Seeing me alone on the road these people opened up with a torrent of the foulest abuse imaginable. Having stood on many a football terrace, I thought I knew most expressions. I obviously didn't. To say that I was shocked is an understatement. I still didn't understand that I had done something unacceptable by walking up Ardoyne Road, but I became frightened by the proximity of the people who did nothing except shout and scream at me. A bit like an animal caught in the headlights of a car at night, I was frozen to the spot. I couldn't go forward or back.

At that moment, I felt a hand on my shoulder. I looked around and a police officer, his face hidden by his helmet, led me away. He suggested that it would be better if I went back in the direction from which I had come. Then he added, 'Be careful.' Had he not intervened and led me away there is no telling how events might have unfolded.

Back at Holy Cross church, I prepared to offer 7.30 a.m. Mass. The prayers included one for all children returning to school that day. People at that Mass had their own concerns that morning as they went off to work or back home to prepare children for school.

Going back up to Ardoyne Road I found that the scene had changed again. There were two large military personnel carriers blocking the road at its junction with Alliance Avenue. The sides of these closed the space between them. In simple terms, the area from which the children would arrive to go to their school was blocked. In front of these vehicles were soldiers with guns. It struck me as strange that these soldiers had their guns facing in the direction from which the parents and children would arrive. It had never been suggested that this was the area from which trouble was likely to arise.

Since my earlier visit, there had been an influx of vans with satellite dishes, radio cars, television crews and journalists. The scene reminded me of something in Downing Street in London, the Dáil in Dublin or the White House in Washington.

By now, it was approaching 8.30 a.m., and the first few parents and children began to arrive from the streets around Ardoyne. Anxiety was written all over their faces. With the road closed, it was difficult to make out what was happening further along.

By prior arrangement, I was to ask for the RUC officer in charge. I was brought in behind the military vehicles to meet the police and some of the military. My sole interest was to find out about the children going to school. The police asked that the parents and children form into one group. Police officers with faces covered, helmets, boiler suits, riot shields and batons would form up on each side.

I could see that the plastic fence had been completed on the left-hand footpath and that police and soldiers were standing around. It did not look a good scene for small children, some going to school for the first time. When the police judged that all was ready, the parents would be ready to move off.

By agreeing to go to school as a 'walking bus', the parents had already voluntarily surrendered a three-decade practice of arriving at school by car or taxi or simply walking. A point sometimes forgotten is that Glenbryn and Holy Cross Girls' School are both part of Holy Cross parish.In fact, until comparatively recently, some Holy Cross parishioners continued to live in Glenbryn. Now the parents and children had to wait in one place until they were allowed by the police to move further up Ardoyne Road.

As final preparations were made to move off to school, an exchange with a group of parents took place that was to alter my life in more ways than I could imagine. These parents asked if I would walk up the road with them. They suggested that this might provide some form of 'insurance' for them and the children. My intention up to that point had been to stay where I was until they got back from leaving their children to school. As the parents and children assembled I asked Fr Gary if he would walk also. He immediately agreed and we decided to walk one on each side. It was at the request of the parents, as primary educators of their children, that, we, the priests, walked with them.

It has been said that on that first morning I asked that only mothers accompany the children to school and that the issue of fathers could be dealt with later. Nothing could be further from the truth. Any parent or guardian, male or female, has an inalienable right to accompany their child to school. Asking a parent not to do so is totally unacceptable. At one stage, the protestors said that they would allow the girls to walk only on the left side of the Ardoyne Road and only with women accompanying them but no nationalist men. These conditions would not be acceptable under any circumstances.

At 8.45 a.m., the group was assembled on the footpath and surrounded by police to walk the short distance to school. Nothing could have prepared us for what happened next. Protestors standing in their gardens unleashed a tirade of abuse against us. This group of people accompanying their children to school was subjected to shouting, spitting, clenched fists, obscene gestures, sectarian taunts, sexual taunts and more.

It was by far the most terrifying atmosphere I had ever experienced. Even the live pictures shown on TV cannot convey the rawness of that morning. At that moment, it seemed to me that we would be fortunate if someone was not killed. It was as tough as that.

It was not that any of the protestors would have contemplated this beforehand, but the appearance of the children going to school seemed to unleash anger and violence that are difficult to imagine. In those circumstances, there was no limit to what could happen.

When Mel Gibson made *The Passion of the Christ*, he captured something of the atmosphere of what the walk of Christ to Calvary must have been like. It was not so much anything that was said; rather it was the foreboding and threatening atmosphere. When I saw those scenes of the film in the cinema the same feelings came back to me from that first morning in September.

My description is that of an adult. To capture the impact on the mind of a child is beyond words. They saw their parents and school friends run a gauntlet of danger and terror. It seemed an eternity before we got to the school gates and stepped inside. Anne Tanney, the school principal, was there to welcome the children back. Before we could move into the school, bottles and bricks started raining down upon us. One lady standing beside me had her head opened by a bottle landing on her – blood streamed down her face.

It became clear that the situation was out of control. Police might disagree but standing there with terrified children and parents, I was convinced that the security forces had got it terribly wrong.

The next issue was to get the children into the school building and safety. There the teachers did what they do so brilliantly – they took charge of the children and brought them to the safety of the classroom. The amazing calmness within the school building was in marked contrast to the mayhem we had just witnessed. Each teacher was in her classroom; Mrs Tanney was dealing with children crying while trying to free herself for a governors' meeting, parents beside themselves with fear and anger, and a growing media corps at the door.

Some parents had not been able to get to the school and must have suffered anxiety as news broke of what was happening. Word spread quickly, and cars and taxis made their way to Crumlin Road to rescue the children and get them home. Most of the children were taken home in a state of sheer terror.

Others, however, did remain in school. Quickly a room was provided for those parents who decided to keep their children in school for the present. The children who were frightened were regularly brought to this room to be reassured that they were safe. Going into a classroom I saw one little girl and her teacher. What a tribute to that teacher to give a familiar, safe and caring environment to that terrified little one. And what a brave little girl – like all who survived that morning's walk to school. The children could hear the noise outside and it must have been a terrifying experience.

The shock of that walk on 3 September will never leave me. Nothing had prepared any of us for the intensity of what took place. It became my dread that we would carry a dead child down that road. I was convinced that if it were to continue, serious injury or death could not be far away. It is not that the people of Glenbryn set out to injure or kill a child. But the potential for violence and for that violence to get totally out of hand was there.

Parents needed to know what was going to happen. Teachers and staff of the school needed some answers too. Not that it was a priority at that moment, but there were reporters asking if the school was closing today and if it would it open tomorrow.

The governors present met in the school staffroom. We had a serious dilemma. If the school remained open, we faced the prospect of further serious violence. Nothing was more important than the safety of the children in the first place. Parents, teachers, staff, protestors and surrounding families on both sides of the divide were important. They could not be left out of our consideration, but our obligation in the first place was to ensure the health and safety of the children.

The alternative course of action was to close the school for a few days and see what could be done to resolve the situation. The difficulty with this latter option was that we most likely would never open the school again. Of course, we still had to weigh this against the danger of injury or death.

As we met, I saw something of the heroism of people in the face of a life-threatening situation. Most of the governors were local people who had lived through three decades of violence. They had seen the best and the worst in people. Other governors who were not from the immediate locality brought to the meeting a rich experience from other parts of Belfast and beyond.

If the situation depended on rational argument alone, I would have despaired of us finding a way forward. But as I looked about the staffroom I knew I was surrounded by solid, good and brave people. They would keep me right, I knew. They were so patient and kind towards me.

With some embarrassment I look back now on one of my first questions to the meeting: 'Will the protest take place again this afternoon?' One of the more experienced present smiled and said yes.

Had the governors been facing an issue about demonstrating against someone or something or marching in support of a cause there could have been only one answer. That would have been to close the school at once. To have done otherwise would have been highly irresponsible.

But we had to remember that this was not the issue. Our sole issue was whether or not to prevent children receiving an education as chosen for them by their parents and provided for by state and church. As I listened to the wisdom of those present, I could see that there was only one answer. We must guarantee that the school be kept open for as long as the parents wished and as the state could ensure the safe passage of the children. We knew that the final decision on this would be taken by the parents. With all due respect, this was not for the protestors to decide.

Already that day, some families had decided that enough was enough and they never sent their children back to the school. They sent them to other schools. Who could blame them? One mother wrote:

My daughter aged seven attended Holy Cross Girls' and has been very happy there. Unfortunately, and it broke my heart to do so, my husband and I felt it was best to move her to a new school. I myself went to this school and I too was happy there. I remember leaving the school in P7 and the sadness I felt then. But it was nothing to the sadness I felt when I took my daughter out of it. But we will have to get over this and as a family I pray that we will come through this nightmare.

A few families decided that there was no future in Ardoyne and moved away completely. Again, who could blame them? These decisions accounted for a decrease in numbers of about fourteen children in the first few weeks of September.

The governors made the decision to keep the school open on the basis of the human right of the child to an education and to the protection of the state in achieving it. We also realised that some children and adults would not be able to face another protest of that morning's intensity. For that reason, and to allow parents the maximum choice, arrangements were made with St Gabriel's College on Crumlin Road to allow any parent and child who wished to reach Holy Cross School to use its grounds. This was a temporary arrangement in response to the danger on Ardoyne Road.

The grounds of St Gabriel's College are tarmac as far as the back of the building. Then a steep grass bank leads onto a football pitch. At the far side of the pitch, there are railings separating it from Holy Cross Girls' School. I am told that this was the route used temporarily in June by the parents and children, following the 19 June disturbances.

It is unfortunate that the unsuitability of this route to Holy Cross School was not filmed in June so that all could see that it was not a viable alternative as some criticised the parents for not bringing their children to school this way. It is true that as the protest continued, Belfast Education and Library Board made great improvements by providing a way over the grass bank and a path for pedestrians, but never at any stage did this become an alternative route to Holy Cross Girls' Primary School.

Once the decision to keep the school open was made, it was communicated. At this stage, we had no way of reaching all the parents as many had already taken their children home. Many learned of the decision by means of news bulletins. Understandably there was criticism of the school governors because of this means of communicating with parents who were entitled to receive the news first. As the days went on, the school endeavoured to improve communication with parents by regular meetings and letters sent home with pupils.

There were many questions from media as to whether it was responsible to keep the school open in light of the events of the morning. There were also questions as to why the front entrance to the school was not closed and St Gabriel's College used as the way to reach the school. It was pointed out that the choice was left to the parents, and whatever they decided would be respected. Had the parents decided to go the long way to school, I would have been happy to accompany them.

However, the immediate reaction of the parents of children still in the school and those I met on the street was that the only way to the school was along Ardoyne Road. The point was also made to me that sending a child to school by what is effectively 'the back door' can give a negative message.

Within an hour of the governors making their decision, I was described by some in the media as the person who had told the parents to go to school by the back door. This label was unfair and untrue. The truth was that I had suggested that the decision of any parents who chose to travel that route would be fully respected by the governors. As ever, it was a matter of parental choice. Also, the intensity of the protest and the danger of serious injury or death made it imperative that the governors address this matter of choice in accessing the school.

Some reports in the days that followed asserted that the parents had defied me in continuing to go to school through the front gate. Nothing could be further from the truth.

In the event, from 3 September until the protest was suspended three months later, some parents chose to bring their children to school through the grounds of St Gabriel's College. Some had to be at work and could not afford to delay until the security forces allowed access along Ardoyne Road.

The decision of these parents was always respected. There was no pressure on them to go that way; there was no pressure on the majority to continue along Ardoyne Road. In some cases, parents confided later on that it was sometimes the child who decided what way they would go to school.

A meeting with some politicians for the Glenbryn and surrounding areas was organised for that afternoon in the school. It was still such a shock to me that I was certain that as soon as these political leaders met with the school governors, there would be a hasty end to the protest. Such was not the case. It became clear that the community issues of the local residents were intertwined with the protest.

Because of the exclusion of the governors from such face-to-face meetings during the summer, this was my first experience of just how wide the gulf was between what the protestors were seeking and our simple plea to let the children go to school in peace. There was a gulf to be bridged. There was a great deal of trust to be built and much wisdom needed to find our way out of this tragedy affecting all the people of this area.

No solution was reached at the meeting that afternoon, and it became clear that the protest would continue. Whether the intensity would be the same was not known. In fact, events before the end of the week would raise the danger and fear to an unimagined level.

However, the meeting with the politicians and representatives ended with one note of progress. As the meeting ended I offered a handshake to the elected representative who had shouted so loudly at me that morning. He shook hands and apologised for any hurt caused. The day was going to end better for me than it had begun.

Looking back now that day is etched in my memory. I can only imagine how the teachers must have felt as the first day back at school drew to a close. The governors had made a decision, the consequences of which were totally unknown and unknowable. Teachers finished their classes and children were brought home safely. But on everyone's lips was the question, 'What is going to happen tomorrow?'

I certainly didn't know. Phone calls from members of the press exceeded anything I could have imagined possible. It never crossed my mind what impact these events might be having not just in Belfast but throughout Ireland, and indeed the world. Much later, I learned of these images being beamed around the world and printed in newspapers in many countries.

As 3 September drew to a close I visited a few families in Ardoyne who had children at Holy Cross School. There was a palpable sense of fear and dread about what lay ahead. This was the beginning of children showing signs of disturbance. Very much on my mind also was the fact that other schools in the area were deeply affected by events on Ardoyne Road. There were brothers and sisters sitting in school fretting about a sister's safety. The teachers and staff of these schools also had to stand strong for the sake of their pupils.

Fr Gary and I got back late to Holy Cross. There were messages and requests from the parishioners that also deserved attention. There were weddings to be prepared, bereaved families to be visited, comforted and assisted in their preparations for funerals, sick calls and other matters to be attended to before the day ended.

Almost like the story of Creation so ended the first day of what was to become known as the Holy Cross protest.

CHAPTER FOUR

OVERNIGHT, THE STORY went around the world. The *Chicago Tribune* carried the story under the heading: 'ALABAMA IN '60s VISITS ULSTER'. The paper reported: 'Most of the pupils – some as young as four wearing brand new uniforms – were sent home early from Holy Cross Primary School. A fleet of Catholic-run taxis ferried them past a line of riot police while many of the Protestants shouted curses and insults.'

In Edinburgh, *The Scotsman* said: 'Any little girl's first day at school is a daunting experience but it is only in Northern Ireland first-day kids must run through a narrow corridor created by policemen in full riot gear and heavily-armed soldiers dodging spit, stones and the foulest abuse.'

These two quotes give a flavour of what the world press was reporting. It could be thought that perhaps it was not as bad as some people said it was, but the sad and tragic truth is that it was worse, and I recall it now not to revive memories or to apportion blame and accusation.

Letters began to appear in the local and international press. A letter from a writer in New Zealand appeared in the *Irish News*, saying: 'Nothing would surprise me when it comes to the deep hatred felt by some people in the North of Ireland, and displayed outside this school [...] The world is indeed shocked and horrified by this. My friends and colleagues here in New Zealand are disgusted and they wonder why these people are not being arrested and charged with assault or attempted murder.'

From Sweden another letter from a person of Lutheran background gave an interesting perspective: 'I feel, together with most people in Sweden, very upset over the actual Protestant demonstration towards young Catholic schoolgirls. How can anyone behave like that against children?? It is almost unbelievable. Think of the image that now is relayed all over the world. Sincerely yours from a professional Lutheran and Protestant.'

Newspapers worldwide carried pictures and stories about the events. As a member of an international religious congregation, I was contacted by colleagues from all over the world, asking what was happening and what could be done to help the children. It was amazing to see the events reported in Italian, Dutch, French, Spanish and other languages.

The goodness of so many people amazed me as cards, letters and messages began to arrive at Holy Cross School and Monastery. There were messages of support and encouragement from parents, schools, clergy, religious communities and so many people I didn't know. So intense were those days that there was scarcely time to read these lovely and supportive messages.

On 6 September the European Committee for Catholic Education in Brussels sent a message to CCMS in Belfast. It expressed shock at the violence as the children went to Holy Cross School. The message expressed sympathy for the children, the families, the principal and the teachers.

On 7 September a statement was issued by Sir Reg Empey MLA, Seamus Mallon MLA, MP and the Rt Hon John Reid MP, pointing out that 'Dialogue is essential between the two communities of North Belfast. Such dialogue can only be effective if exchanges take place in a constructive and peaceful atmosphere.'

Inspired by this call, a discussion paper for consideration was drawn up. Some of the suggestions included the parents going to school not via Ardoyne Road but through the grounds of St Gabriel's College. If this were accepted by the parents, the protest would be suspended. As a symbolic act a child and a parent would be escorted by the police to school along Ardoyne Road.

Another proposal put forward was that the children be bussed up Ardoyne Road while the parents went along Crumlin Road and through St Gabriel's College. There was even a suggestion that local clergy or Holy Cross teachers escort the children to and from school. Another suggestion was that representatives of Glenbryn residents escort the children to and from school each day.

While these proposals were well-intentioned, they missed the essential point concerning the fundamental right of parents to take their children to and from school. The proposals also failed to pay sufficient attention to the core issues of the protestors. There were issues of security, better housing and other social matters brought forward by the Glenbryn community.

Individual people showed great compassion and care for the children, allied to a great desire to see the protest ended for the benefit of all concerned. A priest in Derry, suffering from a serious illness, sent £1,000 to provide a treat for the children. On 4 September, a lady in England wrote:

> I am an Anglican from Surrey. Having seen the news yesterday, I just wanted to demonstrate some solidarity. The appalling behaviour of adults to children! ... I wonder if there is anything I could do? May God stay close to you all.

One of the most surprising messages I received came by phone. The caller did not give a name but in her message she said she was a Protestant from Glenbryn, and she wanted me to know that she was appalled by what had happened on Ardoyne Road. Over the coming months, I came to know that this was true of other residents of Glenbryn.

Among many phone calls received following the events of 3 September was one from President McAleese in Áras an Uachtaráin. As someone baptised in Holy Cross and who had lived in the parish, she wanted to offer assurance of her and her family's prayer and concern at what was happening. Such support was helpful and encouraging. A few days later, a letter arrived from President McAleese in which she wrote:

I was deeply saddened by the heart-rending events of the last week as indeed were countless people throughout the world. The spectacle of little children running the gauntlet of hatred has provoked righteous indignation from every quarter. [...] I know that there are many people of goodwill who are working in partnership across difficult divides to ensure that there will be a peaceful outcome and it is the dignified, courageous actions of these men, women and children which lift our hearts and encourages us to believe that a new constructive, neighbourly atmosphere can be built [...] Please be assured of my prayers and good wishes, as the Catholic and Protestant people of Ardoyne, who hold a special place in my heart, deal with history's awful legacy and face the challenge of creating a happier future. In hope and faith, Mary McAleese, President.

It is interesting to reread the President's letter in the light of a controversy that was to arise in 2005 on the anniversary of the liberation of Auschwitz. It is clear that her concern and prayers were for the Catholic and Protestant people of Ardoyne whom she described as having a special place in her heart.

The night of 3 September, few people in Ardoyne slept well. Apart from the street violence there was the prospect of the next morning and what might happen. Children are resilient and even though no child of any religion should ever see what the Holy Cross girls saw, they arrived next morning with their parents to go to school. Children going to state schools in the area were also being affected by the protest on Ardoyne Road. This was also wrong but there was nothing we as a school or a community could do to lessen their worry.

It is essential to stress that had this been a politically-motivated or paramilitary-fuelled event, I could not and would not once have walked up the road. However, Fr Gary and I knew that as long as it took to support the parental choice to go to school along Ardoyne Road we would be there.

The RUC had seen how disastrously wrong their tactics on the first day had been. Now we had police and army Land Rovers parked on both footpaths along Ardoyne Road. It was an amazing sight to see so many vehicles and personnel lined up on each footpath, creating a corridor that left the road as the only place to walk. Parents were worried about this arrangement as it left the protestors very close and free to shout or throw anything at the children.

They asked me to enquire why the very high screens used in Ardoyne during 12 July parades could not be put in place for the protection of the children. The answer from the police was always the same – the right to protest had to be respected.

This is hard to credit. But as the continuing Judicial Review case taken by one of the parents shows, the Secretary of State and the Police Service of Northern Ireland are still defending that position.

It is interesting to read again a letter from the District Commander, Roger Maxwell, dated 13 September 2001 in which he states:

> an enquiry team to investigate any criminal offences which have occurred from 3rd September 2001 in relation to the Holy Cross Primary School.
>
> In order to assist this investigation I would greatly appreciate if you could use your influence to encourage the parents of the children to contact ourselves if they have any complaints of a criminal nature.
>
> I appreciate the vulnerability the parents will feel when they come forward to provide relevant evidence which may lead to court proceedings. Although I cannot assure anonymity I will, if requested, make an application to the court for particular witness details to be concealed.

This early intervention by the RUC, while well-intentioned, did not yield results. In the first few days of the protest, the intensity and the danger were so overwhelming that the vast majority of the parents did not take up the option of reporting to the police. In time, though, we created an incident book in the school and the contents of this were given to the police at the end of every week. On other occasions, parents made complaints to the police on Ardoyne Road as events unfolded. When eventually parents began to meet the police face to face to deal with school issues I felt that we had made significant progress.

The law of most civilised societies holds that anyone who abuses a child is a criminal. However, the insults, spitting, throwing of bottles and bricks on 3 September did not result in one arrest. When the police were asked why this was so, they replied that arrests could have triggered violence in other parts of Belfast and even further away. If a society is evaluated on how it treats its most vulnerable, such an approach did not auger well for us as we gathered on the morning of 4 September.

The journey to school on that second day of term was different to the extent that we formed a 'walking bus' in the centre of the road. The protestors were as close as the footpath on both sides. The children must have been mystified by the walk to school being through a tunnel of vehicles with heavily armed riot police on both sides. The army vehicles with armed soldiers still faced the parents and children as they arrived for the walk to school.

I was amazed at the attendance that second morning. There was practically a full attendance. As discussed earlier, some parents for both safety reasons and work demands went to school via St Gabriel's College, but the only issue was getting to school.

As we walked towards the school, there was shouting and jeering, and the wet slime of spittle covered many a head. Moreover we had the constant worry that bricks and bottles might be thrown, as on the previous day. The children were kept in the centre of the group with the adults walking on both sides to offer some form of protection.

Having left the children to school, we had to wait until everyone was ready to move back down the road as a group. It was considered far too dangerous for anyone to return down the road without the heavily armed police escort. Even for those who needed to get to work or home, there was no possibility of walking back down the road alone. The abuse continued as we retraced our steps.

Some parents were too nervous to leave their child on their own in school and remained with them the whole day. There was every effort made by the school to make them as comfortable as possible.

The reception class of pupils, under four years of age, left school each day at noon. To offer them some support, I accompanied them for the first few days. The protest was not as intense at this stage but the fear in the hearts of the parents and little ones was just as great.

In the afternoon the parents gathered again at 2.45 p.m. to proceed up the road to collect the children. Again, we could not proceed until allowed by the police. The footpaths were again lined with army and police vehicles, and abusive remarks and abusive language were hurled at the group by the protestors.

It was not long before placards denouncing me as a paedophile began to appear: 'Fr Troy is a paedophile' and other such messages. I am told that some of these appeared quite clearly on TV evening news bulletins. No action was ever taken against those who made these statements. Clear sexual accusations were regularly shouted as Fr. Gary and I passed.

The worrying thing was that the children could hear the noise as the parents made their way up Ardoyne Road. While a parent will suffer great anxiety about their child, a child will also worry about a parent coming through what was a dangerous and upsetting situation.

Even on the second day I still harboured the hope that the protest could not last much longer. I had deliberately not watched the news on TV the night before. For me, this was not a story to be watched but a tragedy to be resolved. Meetings and phone calls had gone on late into the night. Like every other night, I spent some time in the monastery chapel imploring God to watch over the children. Each time I went there, I hoped that the answer of peace would come the next day.

Wednesday, 5 September 2001, will remain with me as a day when I witnessed a miracle. As we made our way to school – children, parents and priests – a bomb was thrown towards us. It exploded before it reached us, injuring police officers and a police dog. The fact that people and an animal were hurt was tragic. The fact that no child was killed was miraculous.

Parents scooped children up in their arms and ran in every direction. I could see Fr Gary directing people towards the school. Some parents were running back down the road away from the school. At this stage, it was not clear if there were other bombs. Anyone I could reach in the confusion, I directed towards the school gates. At least there we would be safe.

It is amazing how quickly we all react under threat of death or serious injury. When eventually the road was clear and everyone had reached the safety of the school grounds, shock hit me such as I had never experienced before. I began to tremble with fear of what might have happened.

An American observer who witnessed these events described them as follows:

> On the third day of school, a blast bomb was thrown by a loyalist youth into the paths of the girls. Four RUC officers were injured by the explosion. A police dog went down as well. No children were physically harmed but that was not yet known to the panicked Catholics running from the total chaos on Ardoyne Road toward the safety of the school gates. Nobody knew what was happening or if they were still in danger.

What effect this bombing of the children has had on them only time will tell. The teachers again were magnificent. Within minutes of arrival, every child was shepherded to her class. The security of the classroom made a stark contrast with the mayhem on the road just minutes before.

Reading the accounts of what happened that morning, I found an opinion offered that the bomb was not meant for the children but that the target was the police. Just as saying that the protest was not directed against the children, that argument just does not stack up.

In fairness to the protestors the point has to be made that it takes only one person to throw a bomb. There is no way of knowing what this person was attempting to achieve. All that can be said is that throwing bombs when children are going to school is totally irresponsible. Not for the first time, I saw the Ardoyne community swing into action. Taxis and cars began to arrive to ferry the children home.

That day, Progressive Unionist Party member Billy Hutchinson stated to the press that he was 'totally ashamed to call myself a Loyalist'. Within hours he would recant this statement.

The events of 5 September shocked me deeply. I was beginning to see how unlikely it was that life would not be lost – that some child would not be killed or at least seriously injured.

As had happened on the previous two mornings, a meeting of the school governors and the principal took place. The fact that we had governors on the road each morning and afternoon says something of their dedication and concern for the children and their education in these extraordinary times.

We were now faced with a crucial decision that I was aware of as being a life or possibly death issue: had the time arrived already to close the school in the face of this madness? The comments of our meeting of 6 August, stressing the possible risks to be encountered by the chair of governors, came back to me.

Nothing in my training or background had prepared me for this. The maps can tell you where Ardoyne is; there were no maps to tell us how to traverse Ardoyne Road in those circumstances.

What kept all of us going were over 200 brave and dependent pupils. We were entrusted with their safety, health and education. If we got it wrong, we would have to carry the burden with us to our graves. I knew that I must listen to those experienced people sitting with me. We began with a prayer for guidance.

We knew that there was an opinion gaining momentum that we should close the school. Indeed, I know of a priest who felt so strongly about this that he went to houses in Ardoyne where a child was attending Holy Cross Primary School and urged the parents to take the child to another school in the area. He acted from the best of motives. However, my firm belief in the Catholic principle of the parent being the one who decides would bring me to disagree profoundly with the actions of this priest. To this day, I believe he was acting disloyally against what the school, parents and Fr Gary and I were doing.

Many possibilities were examined. Arguments for and against closing the school were played out during the governors' meeting. In the end, a decision was reached.

Because of the seriousness of the situation, it was decided that I should write on behalf of the governors to the parents. We were conscious of how upset some parents had been when, on 3 September, they had heard of our decisions through the media.

The letter to the parents is reproduced in full to give some idea of the need we had to explain why we had decided to keep the school open. It read as follows:

Wednesday, 5 September 2001

Dear Parent[s],

In response to the seriousness of this morning's events the Board of Governors of Holy Cross School has held an emergency meeting in the school.

The Board of Governors has responsibility for educating your children in a safe, secure environment and seeks at all times to act in the interests of your children and the school community. We view with grave concern the further deterioration in events but wish to assure parents that we and the staff, with the support of the community, will continue to provide an education for your children in as normal a manner as is possible in these difficult circumstances. We recognise and acknowledge that parents will exercise their best judgement in determining the most appropriate manner for your children to enter this school. We recognise that such judgements will be based on a range of factors including security advice.

Presently we are working with CCMS, the Department of Education and the BELB to develop strategies to address the range of difficulties and educational needs which your children are currently encountering. In this respect we are happy to take on board your views on how best or by what means your children might benefit from additional support.

We wish to assure the community that at all times we place the education and safety of your children uppermost in all our deliberations. We wish to recognise and commend the work of the teachers and staff and the support of parents and the wider community.

Yours sincerely,

Fr Aidan Troy, C.P.

[Chairperson – Board of Governors]

We did not know at this stage if there would be further violence and attacks on the children. Shortly before this letter was composed following the meeting of the governors, we had witnessed a bomb being thrown at the children. A new low had been reached and there were some who suggested that our moral obligation was to close the school in the light of the new level of danger.

The majority of governors had walked the road each day. This was no academic discussion – if we got it wrong, there would be nowhere to hide. We were putting the lives and safety of the children in the forefront of our thoughts. A few weeks previously, I had known nothing of what governors were about. I was learning fast!

Immediately following the throwing of the bomb, a number of Northern Ireland's children's charities united to call for a speedy resolution to the situation at the school. The National Society for the Prevention of Cruelty to Children (NSPCC) strongly affirmed that: 'all children have the right to be educated in a safe and secure environment that is conductive to learning.'

Other children's groups spoke out clearly and strongly in defence of the children and their fundamental right to go to school without harassment.

When eventually the United Nations examined these first few days of the new school term, their report stated:

> During the first ten days of September 2001, front pages of major newspapers carried photographs of terrified and tearful school girls being walked through an adult cordon to their school. One part of the adult cordon was hurling abuse at them, the other trying to shield them.

The report went on to praise the role played by the school but concluded:

> Their victimization has left scars that the school alone cannot heal. [...] Schools should not be left to themselves to protect children from the impact of communal violence or sectarian harassment, with only some additional funding and security. (Professor Katariana Tomasevski, Special Rapporteur on the Right to Education, 6 October 2002)

As referred to above the Northern Ireland Office issued a statement following a meeting between the Secretary of State, John Reid, and Assembly members Reg Empey and Seamus Mallon:

Dialogue is essential between the communities of North Belfast. Such dialogue can only be effective if exchanges take place in a constructive and peaceful atmosphere. We appeal to all concerned to ensure that this is the case. We commend the useful exchanges and initiatives which have been taken by the local community and church leaders in the last few days.

We have had extensive contact with those from the area. There is substantial agreement about the issues to be addressed. There is also widespread acceptance of the need for a formal mechanism for dialogue, which would involve both the Secretary of State and the executive and addressing a full range of social, economic and community issues both now and in the longer term. We believe that this would help to create the environment in which the immediate issues can be addressed.

For an effective mechanism to be created there needs to be careful preparation to ensure that there is confidence across the community. We have therefore asked senior officials to consult immediately with local interests, drawing on relevant experience and expertise.

With three days gone of the first week back to school it was hard to believe that the protest was continuing. By observation alone, it was possible to see the effects the awful events were having on the children and their families.

What amazed me was the attitude of the Northern Ireland Office in speaking about seeking a longer-term solution. There were 225 children under threat morning and afternoon. There was no denying that for years there were social and political issues to be faced and resolved. But how the health and safety of the children could be tied into the solution of these issues amazed me then and still does.

When I asked even in those first few days why more couldn't be done to end the protest and blockade on Ardoyne Road, I heard a phrase that would continue to be repeated – 'there are things happening behind the scenes'. Sincere people were trying but nothing was happening that would rescue the children from the unacceptable way they were forced to go to and from school.

Please God no one will ever again see scenes like those of the first week of September 2001. But if such should happen, then I believe that leaders of church and state must step into the middle of such abuse and see that it is stopped.

The presence of local clergy, politicians and local leaders was contributing to the safety of the children and the prevention of death or serious injury or the outbreak of communal violence. Due credit must be given to those heroic and dedicated people.

But I wonder if the leaders of the four main Christian churches in Ireland had arrived during those first days and walked arm-in-arm up Ardoyne Road, might they have contributed to ending the protest at that point, rather than having it go on for a further three months. Perhaps if the local Member of Parliament, Nigel Dodds (DUP), had walked up the road with his constituents and their children and shown that the protest was as wrong as it was dangerous, it could have contributed to a cessation of the violence.

Both church and political leaders have every right to make their own decisions about where and when they intervene in any situation. Where anyone sees the rights of children being blatantly violated, the need for action more than words becomes urgent. If there were two equally balanced sides contesting some issue, I could understand taking time to reach a resolution. But the lives of children are too important to leave in danger for even one hour, never mind one week.

One evening Cardinal Cahal Daly, retired Primate of All Ireland, phoned to discuss the situation at Holy Cross and to enquire if there was any way in which he could help. His tender care for all involved moved me deeply. The pain in his voice was clear. He was broken-hearted. His phone call lasted little short of an hour. His concern and longing for peace on Ardoyne Road gave me strength and a determination not to rest until the children were taken out of this dreadful situation.

From other dioceses at home and abroad some letters arrived expressing concern and offering encouragement. Among the Irish bishops who made contact in those early days were Raymond Field, Auxiliary Bishop of Dublin, Michael Smith of Meath, Colm O'Reilly of Ardagh and Clonmacnoise, and Edward Daly, retired Bishop of Derry.

Great encouragement was also given by letters from wonderful people such as Dr David Stevens, General Secretary of the Irish Council of Churches. David went on to become leader of the Corrymela Community working for reconciliation. His book, *The Land of Unlikeness – Explorations into Reconciliation,* offers some wonderful biblical and theological perspectives.

Another great figure in the work for reconciliation who expressed her prayerful support was Rev Ruth Patterson, Director of Restoration Ministries. Her *Journeying Toward Reconciliation – A Song for Ireland* examines the possibilities for spiritual healing in the context of so much hurt and mistrust.

Some people took a contrary view. Many phoned me or wrote letters regarding their disagreement with the decisions of the school governors to keep the school open and the parents' decision to continue going to the school. Such opinions are welcomed and are part of any healthy society.

However, the number of people who hide behind anonymity is staggering. As will be seen later, such letters still continue to arrive. The following is just one example – a note with a Dublin postmark which arrived early on in the protest:

Rev Father,

Normal and decent Parents go grey worrying about their kids crossing the street to school. In Belfast they march their babies up the middle of the road into a hail of <u>obscenity</u> and <u>blast bombs</u> for an education and they and you think that's right. But it's not. It's wrong and most of all, it's loveless.

Please show this to the Ladies of Ardoyne. [Emphasis in original]

Needless to say I did not show this to anyone.

The last two days of that first week were repeats of what had gone before. There was no let-up and it seemed impossible that this could last much longer. Little did I know what lay ahead.

Friday afternoon arrived and some walked down the road with a degree of relief that the weekend would give us a break. I certainly shared that sense of relief but I was also deeply saddened by the fact that there was no end in sight – I felt a total failure.

Standing on Ardoyne Road I was talking to some parents when I felt a tug at my sleeve. Looking around, I saw one of the little girls standing in front of me with two boxes of sweets. She handed them to me saying one was for Fr Gary and one for me. She said it was to say thanks for going to school with her each day. Rather foolishly, I thanked the child's mother rather than the child. The mother told me that she had nothing to do with this. On the way down the road the little one said to her mother that she wanted to do this to say thanks.

A moment like that will live in my memory when some of the horrible acts of that first week have dimmed. Here was a child who had refused to be brutalised by all that was thrown at her, her classmates and family.

Now I know for certain that the Kingdom of God belongs to the child. On that Friday afternoon, I realised with clarity why Christ placed a child at the centre of the Kingdom. As the protest went on, I found that these little ones would lead me into a new phase of my life.

The next day I celebrated my first marriage in Holy Cross since my arrival. The couple were so caught up in their big day that they helped me forget for a few hours how horrible life can be and to remember what love can do.

CHAPTER FIVE

IT AMAZED ME how quickly the story of Holy Cross took on a huge media dimension. Prior to this I had no idea how media worked in such circumstances. The office at Holy Cross Monastery and the school received hundreds of calls from news organisations seeking interviews, updates and background material. Late at night or any time after 5 a.m., phone calls were received seeking information.

Some idea of the intensity of media coverage of Holy Cross School during its blockade is revealed in research done by a communications student in 2003. Between June 2001 and February 2003, the *Irish News* and *Belfast News Letter* published a total of 279 articles on the protests, together with 150 photographs and 3 cartoons. The majority of this content appeared in the *Irish News* (172 articles in total, 69 photographs and 3 cartoons.) The *Belfast Telegraph* gave extensive coverage on an almost daily basis.

Papers in the Republic of Ireland covered the events on a daily basis. RTÉ radio and television reported on a regular basis and were present most days on Ardoyne Road. Local crews from Ulster Television and BBC were present most mornings and afternoons. BBC News 24 carried regular accounts that were broadcast around the world and seen by airline passengers.

Sky News covered the events in the first week of September in an extensive way, often going live to Belfast for the children's walk to school. GMTV broadcast its early morning news programme from

Ardoyne Road on a number of occasions.

Some American TV companies also had journalists covering the events. European companies became greatly interested in making programmes as the protest developed. Church-related communications groups took a keen interest in what was happening to the children.

It was clear that the media interest was enormous. There were nights when, in an effort to deal courteously with media enquiries, Fr Gary and I would spend a great amount of time doing nothing but making or receiving phone calls. The number of messages received by Holy Cross Monastery staff had never been experienced before. Besides the media, there were calls to be dealt with from politicians, community leaders, clergy, religious, families around the world and so many good and concerned individuals.

It would be lovely to say that all the calls were positive and affirming. Sad to say, however, such was not the case. There were a few people who thought that it would be good to keep me awake during the night. Many nights the phone would ring every hour from midnight till dawn. In the circumstances, it was not possible to turn off mobiles or the main monastery number. There was still a need to deal with sick calls or other emergencies that might occur during the night.

One of the worst calls to be received was from a male caller who made allegations of sexual abuse against me. This was so worrying that I phoned the police at once. A male and female officer came to see me and could not have done more to assist with my shock and upset. The caller would not give me a name, address or contact phone number. A trace was put on the telephone line to try to identify the caller should he phone again. No other call ever came but each time I picked up the phone, especially at night, there was the fear that the same allegation might be made. The original call had come from a pay-as-you-go mobile phone which was not easily traced.

Fr Gary and I were totally unprepared for this aspect of what was happening. The guiding principle that I had with regard to media was that I would not pick and choose to whom I would speak. In that way I tried to be fair to anyone who contacted me about events. The cost was far greater than I could ever have imagined in terms of hours given to interviews.

The Tablet magazine, published in England, asked me to write an article about events at Holy Cross. At first, I refused by pleading a lack of time. It was Fr Gary who encouraged me to write it as he felt it important to tell the story to Christians in other parts of the world. He was absolutely right.

It was with surprise and some amusement that I was contacted by RTÉ's *Late Late Show* in Dublin. While respecting Pat Kenny and the show, I was concerned that *my* appearance would somehow take from the single issue of getting the children safely to and from school. At first, I refused and mentioned this to some parents. Their reaction surprised me. It was their advice to accept this offer on the basis that the story of Holy Cross needed to be told throughout the whole of Ireland.

When I did accept the invitation, I was amazed at the warmth of the audience and the number of people who contacted the school or me afterwards, offering their help and support. This was a whole new world to me and one that I had never imagined would be part of my life.

As a student in Mount Argus, Dublin, in the 1960s, I had attended two courses at the Communications Institute at Booterstown Avenue in Dublin. During my years of study and ministry, I had become aware of the influence media can exercise. This came home to me especially during the schools retreats in which I was involved from the early 1970s until today. But there is a difference between being convinced of the influence of media and being involved on a daily basis. This was a choice that I made, and I know that some of my colleagues in the hierarchy and clergy would have wished I had said less. Truthfully, my sole interest in this whole area was to help the children be freed from the abuse they were suffering.

A well-meaning PR company arrived within days of the return to school in September, offering to take over the whole area of media relations. This group came with a recommendation from an Irish bishop. My reaction was to be appalled that we should go down this road. This was, and remains, essentially a justice issue of families educating their children as they choose.

There were some who would have seen many advantages in accepting this offer, which came free of charge. My strong reaction against such a move was my fear that any putting of 'spin' on the events at Holy Cross might eventually work against the clarity of the fundamental issue and could even have worked against the children. At a Board of Governors' meeting on 10 September, the proposal of the PR company was discussed and it was agreed unanimously not to take up the offer.

At no stage did the school appoint an official spokesperson. It was decided that the school governors would talk principally to the parents and only then to media groups. Further, it was decided that the teachers and staff would be screened from publicity by Anne Tanney speaking on their behalf. It was also occasionally necessary to speak on behalf of Holy Cross parish and to address parishioners on matters affecting our lives as a Christian community.

Thus, there was no control exercised by the governors on relationships with the media. In their own way, the ladies and gentlemen of the media were courteous and pleasant in any dealings I had with them. The only complaint I had was the late and early hours at which they could phone!

It was recognised by the governors that there was a need to improve communication with the Right to Education group. The crucial role of this group was recognised, as was the importance of both groups working closely together to agree and focus on the key issue of the children. Following the governors' meeting of 10 September, the offer was repeated for two governors to join the RTE group.

Over the weekend of 8 and 9 September Holy Cross had become a major news story. Headlines from local and international papers spoke of 'To school through the shields' and 'To school through a tunnel of hate' (*Irish Independent*, 8 September 2001). The television channel with the widest global audience, CNN, ran hourly updates on the situation which it said had forced 'Ireland's children to run a gauntlet of hatred on their way to school'. The French newspaper *Libération*, ran a headline: 'In Belfast, war begins at school'. Its competitor, *Le Figaro*, wrote of 'The deep hostility that starts in Belfast's schools'. An Italian daily paper, *La Répubblica*, described events in Ardoyne under a picture of a five-year-old girl in tears. The full-page feature drew comparisons with 15-year-old black American, Elizabeth Eckford, who made history in the 1950s when she fought her way through the

National Guard to an all-white high school in Arkansas.

The *Sunday Business Post*, on 9 September, ran a two-page feature under the title 'Terror at Holy Cross'. In an editorial comment, the paper addressed directly an issue that has persisted to this day – namely, the blaming of the parents for taking their children through a corridor of hatred, thereby risking their lives and health, both physical and psychological. There were and are many who subscribe to this opinion. They have a right to their opinion and it must be respected.

But the difficulty with this opinion is that it denies a parent, because of their religious affiliation, the right to make decisions about their children's education. If the parents had, for example, taken their children through violence and street disorder completely unrelated to education, this argument might have much to recommend it.

However, in this instance, many of the children were bewildered when asked which way they wanted to go to school. The older ones in particular wanted to go to school the way they had gone for the previous number of years. These children were not interested in what the rows between adults were about.

It is the right of anyone to protest. It is not the right of anyone to intimidate small children. It took heroic parents to stand up to violence and threats to their own and their children's lives.

At a meeting following the throwing of the bomb, when the school governors announced that the school was remaining open, the decision received a standing ovation. In an economically deprived area like Ardoyne, where only 3 per cent of the population have a third-level qualification, parents place a high value on education – it can be a powerful passport to a better life.

Furthermore, these parents love their children more than any political cause. Of course, Ardoyne is strongly nationalist and republican on one side and unionist and loyalist on the other, but this does not mean that parents don't love and cherish their children more than their politics. Besides, it is untrue and extremely offensive to imply that the parents abused their children by walking through a protest over which they had no control.

The other motivation that cannot be forgotten is that parents knew that Holy Cross Girls' Primary School has a most dedicated and caring set of teachers and staff. The children loved their teachers more as friends than as authority figures to be feared (as was the case in my own day!) The majority of these teachers and staff had to travel into Ardoyne daily and leave for home each evening. For the duration of the protest, they did not know if teaching would be possible or if they would simply dry tears and hold trembling children. They, in fact, did both equally well.

It is interesting that from 3 September until the suspension of the protest, not one teacher phoned in to say she was sick or could not come to school for some other reason. It is nothing short of insulting to suggest that these highly motivated and professional people were party to an abuse of children by their parents. The silence of these teachers about the protest should not indicate that they somehow had no opinion about the protest.

It was my privilege to meet with the teachers both formally and informally. The weakest part of the governors' care for the whole school lay in our neglect of discussion and consultation with the teachers. Anne Tanney did this in a superb way as principal. However, the governors could and should have done more to consult and support the teachers. If an excuse can be offered for our failure, it can only be put down to the intensity of getting the children and parents safely to and from school each day.

During the protest, an American author interviewed me for a book she was writing about people who acted in an outstanding way in support of their community. When she had completed her interviews, she told me that my story would not be included. This was no surprise to me. She should have interviewed the parents and the children – then she would have had true heroes and outstanding examples of what a community under threat can do.

There is an aspect to what took place in the first week of the protest that seemed to merit little comment. That is the morality of what was taking place. In political language there is not much room for words like sinful, giving scandal to God's little ones, acting contrary to the Beatitudes, and so forth. But each day on Ardoyne Road, I was aware that evil existed. This is not to say that the protestors were evil and all the Holy Cross parents and children were angels. As already acknowledged, the real issues of fear and concern of the Glenbryn residents needed examination. That the actions of people can be evil is what concerned me. If I had no concern for the protestors, then such an issue would not arise. For me, they also are children of God and must be held as precious because made in His image and likeness. It would be wonderful if this aspect could be put more gently or even ignored altogether. But any respect for truth does not allow the sin dimension to be ignored. I realise that some people will dismiss this, saying that a Catholic priest *would* say that because of his training and calling.

Already within the first week, I glimpsed something of the depth of bitterness that existed on Ardoyne Road. Even though sectarianism is not limited to one community, there is no denying that this protest was fuelled by anti-Catholicism. It would be cowardly not to state this and equally it would be wrong to leave such a comment without seeing how the issue of sectarianism might be addressed, and I will come to that later.

However, at the end of that first week, I was only beginning to sense the depth of hatred that otherwise good people were showing towards the children and the parents.

The name of Christianity was not coming out with any merit from what was happening. One night in a restaurant in Belfast, a man spoke to me. He was a Protestant from the Shankill Road, out celebrating his birthday with his daughter. He spoke of sadness about what was happening and shook hands as a sign of his total abhorrence of any and every form of sectarianism. There are so many good people around and a gesture like that was a sign of hope in an otherwise bleak situation.

Recalling the events of September 2001 and the months of the protest that would follow is very different from the daily living of them as they unfolded. The only objective was to get the children out of this abusive situation and return the school to normal. Many good and intensive efforts were made over the weekend by local politicians and community leaders on both sides to bring about an end to these awful events. That the second week was sure to be the last we would see of these horrible events was my hope. One week earlier I had asked if the protest would be on in the afternoon; now I was talking in terms of weeks rather than days. Little did any of us know that it would turn out to be months before the protest was suspended and years before the school would cease to be targeted.

When, on Sunday, 9 September 2001, I was asked to be part of a discussion on *Sunday Sequence* on Radio Ulster, I was concerned that somehow the events of the previous week had become more of a story than a basic matter of children going to school. My hope was that through a sharing of views among panellists, some progress might be made.

A major breakthrough did come when a meeting was brokered between a group representing the Concerned Residents of Upper Ardoyne (CRUA) and a group of school governors. There was apprehension as the meeting assembled in a local centre. Each side listened with courtesy as the other put forward its views. It was a huge advantage to be meeting face-to-face in such a reasonable manner. The governors had a burning desire for this meeting to succeed. Our only ambition was to get the children back to normality.

The CRUA group also wanted this meeting to succeed in order to spare them any further adverse publicity and to bring about some progress with their community issues. Well might any reasonable person ask why we did not succeed at this stage in resolving the differences between us. Here we were, sitting in the same room and talking to each other. Each participant will have their own view on why this meeting did not end the protest. The group from Glenbryn was required to bring back any proposals to a meeting of its own committee and also put them to the whole community of Glenbryn at a full meeting the following weekend. The school governors also had to be mindful that we were there on behalf of the parents and the school.

But these factors alone do not explain why we failed to resolve the difficulties. The biggest obstacle that I could see was that the governors were not free to negotiate anything while the children were still being prevented from going to school in peace. If we had, we would have betrayed them and their parents' right in their education. During the discussion, there were calls for reciprocation. This became a word used widely by CRUA, some unionist politicians and some Protestant clergy. The problem was that the children had nothing to give. They had done nothing wrong. To make them bargaining chips would have been immoral. As we saw it, all issues could be dealt with once the protest was suspended and the children safe once more. But because of the lack of any trust between our two groups this could not be done for fear that the issues affecting Glenbryn would not be addressed. This was total stalemate.

Nevertheless, this first meeting was courteous and without rancour. In fact, towards the end of the meeting a member of the CRUA delegation asked me about the sign on the religious habit that both Fr Gary and I wore as we walked to school. This gave me an opportunity to ask if the way we dressed in religious attire was a cause of irritation to the protestors. If this had been a contentious issue, it would have been possible to leave aside all religious symbols in an effort to spare the children further suffering. He assured me that the religious habit was not an issue.

The sign about which the CRUA delegate had asked is heart-shaped with a white cross in the centre. On the sign, in Hebrew, Greek and Latin, is written 'The Passion of Jesus Christ'. Within the heart is a representation of the three nails of the Christ Crucified. This sign was given to St Paul of the Cross, founder of the Passionist, in a vision of Our Lady as he prepared to found his new Congregation in 1720. It is the distinctive mark of Passionists.

Somehow I could not but be struck by the strangeness of the situation as the whole group listened to this explanation. The man who had asked the question smiled. I asked him was there anything else he wanted to know. He assured me that this was fine and said he was pleased to be able to bring back an answer to this question to some others who had asked. The following day, this same man was on the street as vocal as ever among the protestors. At least he knew what Fr Gary and I were wearing on our habits.

Yet communication did not die. Heroic efforts were made to find ways to reach some middle ground from which we might make some progress. Much to my surprise, one morning an RUC officer conveyed to me that a group of Glenbryn female residents wished to meet me. He said that they were standing nearby, and, if I agreed they would meet me immediately. I was delighted with this unexpected turn of events. The officer suggested that if I walked back up Ardoyne Road towards the school, the ladies would make themselves known to me. Shortly after I had set off up the road, a group of six or seven came towards me.

Immediately one or two of them uttered a few abusive words about me and the actions of the parents and school during the protest, and then left. Those who remained were ready to begin. The main reason for these ladies asking to meet me was to enquire why I told so many lies about them in the media. Upon enquiry, they said that I was constantly telling lies to put the whole community in a poor light throughout the world.

One example they gave me was about the protestors throwing balloons filled with urine and excreta at the children as they went to school. My response was to say that I had witnessed and experienced this event myself. Immediately they responded by saying that once again I was repeating another lie. Not being an expert in psychology, I have no wish to analyse this conduct. It seemed to me that these people were in denial and this struck me as being dangerous. Another example was their total denial that hot tea was thrown at the parents and children.

We continued to talk in a civil way for approximately forty minutes. One of the women asked me would I join them in their 'community house' of Glenbryn for coffee. Nothing would have pleased me more as an effort to build trust, but when I looked toward the house to which I had been invited, I could see there was a group of men from the protest standing around the door. Sadly, I judged it better not to accept the offer.

When I got back to the police officer who had remained not far away he enquired how things had gone. I thanked him for whatever role he had played in making the chat on the road possible. I mentioned the offer of coffee and his opinion was that I had made the right decision. Whether this is so or not, I will never know.

Another offer of dialogue also came about one morning when a group of residents came to speak to Fr Gary and me at the entrance to the school. Again, there was a serious effort made to engage and I found a great value in listening to what was said. The conclusion of that conversation centred on the threat to the families in Glenbryn from the republicans in Ardoyne. One person said that her home had recently been wrecked in an attack coming from Ardoyne. When I asked if it would be possible for me to visit the home and see for myself what had happened, the initial response was positive. But when I took out a pen to write down the address, the response was no. This was another instance of how trust was at a premium – I would not go for coffee and others would not trust me with their address.

These events helped me to see how little we trusted each other. Only with the building of trust would it be possible to engage with each other as people do in more normal situations.

To build trust involves taking some risks. At a second meeting between the school governors and representatives of the protestors, organised by local politicians, it appeared that not much progress was being made. It seemed like a repeat of our first meeting. As the meeting concluded, I asked if there was anything that could be done to maintain contact with one another. It was becoming clear that the protest would not have a swift conclusion.

In an effort to keep channels of communication open, I offered my mobile phone number to the man who had previously asked me about the Passionist habit and sign. It was clear that some of my fellow governors felt uneasy at this, and they pointed out to me afterwards that there were risks involved. However, I can truthfully say that never once has this trust ever been abused. In fact, on a few occasions, being able to keep in contact was a key factor in preventing further trouble. Moreover, once I had been contacted the first time, I now had a mobile phone number to make contact with one of the protestors.

None of this, however, brought an end to the suffering of the children. A local doctor expressed his alarm at the number of young children who were in need of medication for anxiety-related illness and to help them to sleep. This was a frightening development and one that caused great concern to the parents.

Besides these efforts to engage, there were meetings on a regular basis with the parents to keep exploring how we might move forward. It was my conviction that if this protest ever became separated from the parents and their commitment to education, there was a real danger of serious violence. There are people who still believe that this was a politically motivated exercise that used the children. If Fr Gary or I had ever suspected or known such was the case, our walking to and from school would have ended.

Every time I was invited to address the parents at a meeting, I could see at once the suffering and concern written on their faces. These people had come through some tough times themselves but this was something completely different. Children were in danger and it was looking more and more likely that we were in for a protracted protest.

And yet, each day we went to school amid the most awful obstacles, and the children settled into class, and the teachers and staff kept the school operating in a most normal way. Each day, there were visitors to offer support and to express concern. The one comment they all made was how normal things were in school in an otherwise abnormal situation.

The need to support each other was as vital as the efforts to reach out to the protestors. One day, early in September, a group of mothers remarked how lonely it was when they got back to their own homes. They would spend their time worrying if their child was all right and wondering what the next walk to the school would hold. They needed some place to meet and talk and share their stories and concerns with each other.

In Holy Cross Monastery there is a large room which, when there were twenty-five members in the community, was used by the Passionists as a television room. With only a handful now in Holy Cross, this room was no longer suitable for that purpose. A short chat with the community and we had this room ready for the use of the parents every morning after they left the children to school. A hot-water boiler and a few cups were all that was needed to get started. This developed into a key area for many of the parents for the next few months.

This new use for this room caused concern for some of the Passionist community. On a few occasions, a buggy with a baby would be seen on the corridor while a mother prepared a bottle. This was a new experience for us!

While Fr Gary and I were on the road every day and some nights, there were colleagues back at Holy Cross Monastery who were part of our efforts to protect the children. We were very grateful for the generosity of other members of the community who assumed extra duties when events at the school kept us outside. Another wonderful support was the regular meetings of the Passionist community to reflect on the events that were happening in our midst and to pray together for a speedy resolution.

It should be acknowledged that by this early stage, the Department of Education had released funding towards a relief package for the school. While this would not solve the impasse, at least we were not under financial pressure in an otherwise awful situation.

As the second week of the protest got under way an event was to occur that changed the world. It was the bombings in America with such terrible loss of life and the fear that our world had become a less safe place to live. I was walking back from school on Tuesday, 11 September, relieved to have reached the safety of Alliance Avenue, when I was invited to sit into a van belonging to Sky TV. There I was shown pictures that looked like something from a science fiction movie. Aeroplanes were crashing into the Twin Towers in New York. These I was told were pictures being transmitted of events that had just happened.

As I sat there dumbfounded, I was certain that this was the end of our local dispute. Surely there could be no continuation of what we had witnessed over the previous week in the light of what had just happened to our brothers and sisters in the United States.

The next morning, before we moved off to school, the parents and children joined in a prayer and a minute's silence before approaching the military and police barricade on Ardoyne Road. There was a hush and an atmosphere of quiet among our group as we set off up the road to school. But it is sad to say that we were not met with a similar atmosphere among the protestors. Instead, there was jeering to the effect that the Americans would not be sending any more dollars to their republican friends. I was deeply saddened to hear this and hoped that there would be a change of heart.

A day later, a prayer service was held by the protestors before we passed to school to remember those who had died in America. Even in the most bitter of conflicts, it was good to see that our grief was as one.

Had the protest been suspended following 11 September, the gesture would have been loudly applauded by all people of goodwill. However, that did not happen.

But one consequence of the events of 11 September was that the world press moved away as the events in New York and Washington took on a worldwide significance. This relieved some of the pressure that could arise from having such extensive coverage of the children. In the early days, it was necessary to ask camera operators not to slow us down as we walked to school. They were never anything but co-operative.

As we moved towards the middle of September, there was no end in sight. Many people continued to assure me that there were things happening 'behind the scenes'. The sad truth is that there weren't.

CHAPTER SIX

IT IS DIFFICULT to believe how the protest sought to degrade the children and the parents as they walked to and from school. Mention has already been made of the bricks and bottles hurled on the first day and the bomb a few days later, but every day there was the taunting and name calling. Some of it was of a very degrading nature and referred frequently to 'fenians', 'bastards', 'bitches', 'paedophile priests', 'stupid whores' and some that I would not want printed. By wearing walkman headphones, some of the children were spared some of the horror of hearing their parents being pilloried in this way.

The shrillness of the whistles blown as we walked past was added to by other sources of noise. For some weeks one of the protestors attached horns to a car battery and strapped them to a supermarket trolley. This made it possible for him to walk alongside the children and parents from the school gate to the end of the road, blaring the noise all the way. Before the protest, my hearing was as good as perfect; now I have a medical opinion that all is not as it once was. This is a minor detail in comparison to the damage done to young children's ears.

On occasion, the police were asked if they could arrest or at least caution the person persecuting the children in this way. Their response was always that they could not arrest him but that they would speak to him. After his talk with the police, he was back the next day creating as much noise as the day before.

Pornographic pictures were held up by some of the protestors, often women, as we walked past. There was no effort made to remove those holding these pictures or those who shouted about sexual perversions of parents or priests. My hope is that the children were not too deeply harmed by these images, which nobody could avoid seeing.

The day that balloons were thrown over the heads of the group walking to school, it was thought at first that this was some sort of joke. It was far from it! These balloons were filled with urine, and the smell alone was enough to make it clear what was happening. A child reeking of urine could not be left to sit in school in soaked clothes. Again, apart from the repulsive nature of this, there was the annoyance and inconvenience caused.

Every day I kept my eyes on the children and the parents. Sometimes, when asked later about something happening among the protestors, I had to admit that I had not seen it, as I seldom looked at who was there. Of course, it was impossible not to see some faces and to hear what was being shouted as we passed. On some occasions, masks were worn by the protestors, and it amazed me how this increased the level of fear among us. It was difficult to remain unaffected by the masks, some of which were of well-known politicians and of horror film characters.

Amid the horrible events there were moments when it was the children who sustained the adults. One afternoon, a little girl told me that her mother had not arrived to take her home, and she needed some adult to walk with her. She asked me to walk her down the road with the others who had adults with them. Even though she had known me for only a few days, her trust was absolute. It broke my heart to see those little eyes look up at me as she held out her small hand for me to take. I had to explain to her that she was so precious that I would need someone else to help me as I would have to move about a bit as we went down the road. That was all right with her. One of the mothers understood and helped with protecting this little one.

The truth was that it was out of the question for me to hold the hand of a child. The reputation of clergy in Ireland and around the world has suffered enormously over sexual abuse offences. The betrayal of trust is something not easily forgiven. The protestors frequently shouted accusations that we priests were interfering with the little children or even slurs about our being the father of a child.

In sharp contrast was the unwavering trust in their priests shown by the parents and children. In all my years as a priest, never had I known such steadfast trust. Out of the circumstances of the protest, bonds of love and friendship were born that no power on earth can break. It became clearer to me each day how heinous a crime it is to betray trust.

The priority remained to work for the ending of the protest. As long as the protest lasted, the daily challenge was to ensure the safety of the children and their parents on the road, and the safety of the teachers and staff. Most evenings and nights were spent at some form of meeting, searching for a way to end this nightmare. People of all denominations and none were diligent in working for this.

It came as a shock when, one afternoon, the RUC officer in charge took me aside and told me that a message had been received by a TV newsroom that there was a sniper on Ardoyne Road waiting for us to go to the school. The officer added that if the parents were to proceed up Ardoyne Road, someone could be shot. The parents would have to be told of this before he could allow them to pass the military vehicles and begin the walk to collect their children from school. He gave me a stark choice – would he tell the parents or would I? He needed an immediate answer and it seemed better for me to do this and see what the parents would decide in the light of such a serious threat.

I knew at once that I was going up the road in any case. This was not because of a desire on my part to die or to be a hero, but quite simply because there were 225 children, some parents, teachers and school staff already in Holy Cross School awaiting our arrival. It was clear to me that if nobody went up to school that afternoon, the school would effectively be closed forever. All it would take in the future was some such threat and the school would have to close. Furthermore, my information was that if Holy Cross Girls' School closed, there were at least three other Catholic schools in North Belfast that would be targeted by the loyalist community (not just in Glenbryn) for closure.

I asked Fr Gary to help get the parents into small groups so that we could discuss the threat and reach a decision. Before talking to each group, I asked the media present not to record or film these conversations. Although they already knew what was happening, to their credit they did as I requested.

It was a difficult decision. Clearly, no school building of bricks and mortar is worth the injury or death of one person. Each group was told of the threat posed by the sniper and each conversation ended with me saying that I was going up the road to the school. It was a moving experience when each group said that if that was my decision, then they were walking up the road also. Moments like this are etched in my memory. This kind of solidarity gave me strength and a determination to serve and support these people in the best way possible.

The police officer was told of our decision. It posed a danger for the police also as they would be walking alongside us, although they, of course, were wearing protective clothing which might save them in the event of bullets being fired. We set off in silence and, to be truthful, my knees were knocking. I totally believed the warning and was waiting for a shot to ring out.

As we walked up Ardoyne Road, we were greeted by silence from the protestors. This had a most unnerving effect. It dawned on me that if the sniper fired, serious questions would be asked about why I had not urged people to avoid such danger. I hoped and prayed that if anyone was to be shot, it would be me rather than a mother or father. Our walk up the road seemed to take an eternity. But at last we got to the sanctuary of the school and again I could see the relief on the parents' faces as they collected their children. And then there was the walk back down the road in the hope now that all would be safe.

At no time was it suggested by the police that we should wait until a thorough search had been made by them among the protestors and the streets along the route. If this had been done, it would have shown that the fault lay not did with a group of parents, but precisely in the blockade of their legitimate route to school. While the individual police officers generally acted in a courteous manner, the weight of blame was clearly being laid on the parents. As someone recently arrived into this situation, I could not grasp how this was being allowed to happen.

As October loomed it saddened me to see the protest enter a second month. After the sniper threat, a tactic often used by the protestors was to throw fire crackers on to the road. These fireworks come into great use at Halloween and could be heard late into the night.

There were also moments of levity when the protestors would choose a theme to go with the protest. In honour of the arrests in Colombia, we were treated to the spectacle of Latin American clothes and music. We could not but smile and wonder if there was any way we could reach out and ask why we must go on with this madness

One day, in desperation, I asked the police officer in charge if I could walk up the road on my own before the bigger group came, and ask the protestors if there was even one person who would step out from the crowd to speak with me. It was a serious request, but it was made because of my belief that there were men and women among the protestors who were looking for an end as much as we were. It was my hope that if even one or two people were prepared to take that step, we might have a ray of hope. My proposal was ruled out as not possible on security grounds.

At one meeting with the police an offer was made of an unmarked armour-plated RUC bus to bring the children to and from school. The offer was made in good faith but revealed the gap in understanding by the police about the nature of what was happening. To accept the bus would have been an acceptance that the fault lay with the choice of the parents to access this parish school. It would have been only a matter of time until the school would be forced to close.

I know that, in the unlikely event of children of another religion or none being targeted on their way to school through Holy Cross parish, every member of the monastery would have felt obliged to stand out in front of the protestors and name what was happening as evil. It is such a tragedy that the witness of Christians was so damaged as we saw neighbours who carry the name of Christ so divided and children caught up in a dispute that was not of their making and not possible for them to resolve.

However, hope was crucial all along. It was at the heart of my morning and night prayers. I dreaded to think of what might happen if hope went. The strength came from God through the children and the parents. Meanwhile, the teachers kept teaching – the staff kept the school operating to its high standard.

The daily presence on the walk to and from school of two members of the Northern Ireland Human Rights Commission was a source of encouragement and support for us. Started under the Good Friday Agreement, the Human Rights Commission has the potential to put justice and the protection of rights on a sound and proper footing. Little did we know at this stage that the Holy Cross School protest would become part of the serious wounding of the Commission, as will be discussed later.

The two commissioners who walked so faithfully and became so supportive cannot be too highly praised. The career of one of these people was adversely affected by the bravery of his actions. His actions in support of the children's and parent's rights contributed to his losing his position as CEO of a church-based charitable organisation.

On 18 September 2001, there was a glimmer of hope when Anne Tanney and I were asked to meet the Sectary of State at Hillsborough Castle. There could be only one item on the agenda and that was how best to protect the children and ensure the enforcement of their right to go to school. Already the Northern Ireland Office had made contact through MPs Jane Kennedy and Des Browne. That evening an NIO car and chauffeur arrived in Ardoyne to drive us to Hillsborough.

As we moved out of Belfast, there was a chance that we could come back with a breakthrough. The car was waved through the gates of the castle and came to a halt near the front door. As we emerged from the car, a piper struck up. He was going to pipe us inside. To say that we were surprised by this welcome is something of an understatement. Hurriedly an official rushed out the front door and the notes of the bagpipes trailed away. We were not the VIP guests after all! We were ushered in through a side door.

Dr Reid gave us a warm welcome and a tour of the castle. Then it was down to business and a thorough exchange took place. What was absent was a commitment to address the immediate need to get the children safely out of the protest. All the time there was the balancing of rights. The children's right to education and the right to protest were being balanced. The problem was that the right to access their school was being put in second place to the right to protest.

Also there was an implied agenda that the enforcing of the

children's right to education would mean the tackling of a large number of protestors. The next day, 19 September, eight Glenbryn residents were arrested for public order offences. They were released on bail and went back to the protest at once. No one was ever convicted for their conduct between 19 June and the suspension of the protest at the end of November. Later, when a judicial review action was taken by one of the parents against the police and the NIO it emerged that there is an unwillingness to admit that the children were innocent victims.

The Conservative shadow Northern Ireland Secretary, Quentin Davies, visited Holy Cross on a few occasions. On his first visit, he asked me to walk Ardoyne Road with him. He found it hard to believe that he and I could not walk a road within the United Kingdom as we chose. He was soon to learn. Some, seeing him walking with me, taunted him as a 'fenian' and told him to go back to where he belonged. To his credit he gave time and listened closely to what was said to him by parents and staff. On another occasion, he came to visit the work of restoration of Holy Cross Church. Months later, much to my surprise, I was contacted by his secretary at Westminster to invite me to a meal with him in a Belfast restaurant. When we met, there were just the two of us and he told me that he wanted to meet me socially and not just in the context of dealing with problems. We had a most interesting evening of conversation.

The Liberal Democrats shadow Northern Ireland Secretary, Lembit Opik, MP for Montgomeryshire, who was born in Northern Ireland, also visited Holy Cross to express his own concern and that of his party. The Labour MP Kevin McNamara kept in close contact and sent some of his assistants on a regular basis to Ardoyne.

Ruth Kelly MP was born in County Derry but her family decided to move to England because of the effect the Troubles were having on their business. She is currently Secretary of State for Education in Tony Blair's Westminster cabinet. Shortly after the return of the children to school two of her researchers came to Holy Cross to assess what was happening. Her appreciation of the way her emissaries were received in Ardoyne was conveyed in a letter from the House of Commons on 24 September 2001.

Another source of support and encouragement came from the United States. Individuals, parishes, schools, the Ancient Order of Hibernians (AOH), Irish American Unity Conference, Doors of Hope and many other groups and individuals made contact simply to express their concern and seek ways to help.

Schoolchildren around the world were among those who expressed great concern. One school in the west of Ireland wrote in most moving terms about the sorrow of its pupils and staff and their worry when they saw the pictures from Holy Cross. Other schools wanted to let the children know that their suffering was a source of pain to them also.

Good people offered invitations to the children and parents to visit them for a break. Among the many that arrived was one from Basil Keogh of Peacock's Hotel at Maam's Cross in Connemara. A wonderful weekend was spent there by a group of parents and children when the protest was suspended. The night before the arrival of the children, there was a fire at the hotel, and it was immediately suspected that this had been started because of the imminent arrival of the children next day. However, the truth was far simpler in that the preparations for the annual 'Bogman's Ball' were responsible!

During this visit to Connemara, clergy of other churches were in the welcoming party to greet the children. A local school provided a colourful welcome in song and dance. Local musicians played enthusiastically and a disco for the children provided a memorable start to what turned out to be a wonderful visit. Gaeltacht Minister Éamon Ó Cuív came from Dublin to be there to welcome the parents and children.

On another occasion, a group of children and parents were flown to Dublin to spend a weekend there. On arrival at Dublin Airport, the children were brought to the top of the Smithfield Tower where they were greeted by An Taoiseach, Bertie Ahern. From the time of my arrival in Holy Cross, regular and helpful contact was made by Irish government officials and maintained on a weekly basis. It was important to know that this concern was there all the time.

The Finucane Centre in Derry organised a Halloween Fun Day for the pupils. Ardoyne Pubs and Clubs Association also paid for a party for the children and a night of celebration for the parents. This group also presented the school with a cheque to help the children at a time of suffering.

Individuals and families from various parts of Ireland and elsewhere made offers to take a family in particular need to spend time with them for a rest. Irrespective of where the offers of help came from during those months, I was deeply impressed by the sheer thoughtfulness of so many 'strangers'. This is a concrete example of the Body of Christ, with members caring for each other. In truth, prior to these events at Holy Cross I would not have thought of making contact with people facing a crisis or in the wake of some tragedy. The sheer goodness and thoughtfulness of so many people has left an abiding impression on me.

From the beginning of my involvement at Holy Cross, many individuals and organisations have kept in regular and helpful contact. Groups like the AOH have been instrumental in bringing children, parents and teachers from Holy Cross to the United States.

Perhaps the event that most captivated us all was the invitation to be present at Áras an Uachtaráin for the lighting of the Christmas tree in December 2001. The journey to Dublin was an adventure for all – pupils, teachers, governors and everyone who travelled. A lunch at Castlebellingham with entertainment provided gave our party a great chance to relax and enjoy this day out. President and Dr McAleese, together with the staff at Áras an Uachtaráin, could not have done more to make us welcome. Their comment was that the children were so beautiful and well-behaved.

So many wonderful people rallied to the support of the parents and children. A huge post arrived every day. The vast majority of the messages were very positive and encouraging but some, such as the following, took a different view:

As a parent I wonder are the children of Holy Cross getting a fair deal not from the protestors but from their own parents and the school. As parents we should not allow our children to be in a situation where they can be spat at, cursed at, jeered at and terrified. Get the Northern Ireland Office to build you a proper back entrance. Lovely as it may seem pleasant tuneful hymns in the school hall will not be compensation long-term for the damage the children are suffering now. [Anonymous: A Catholic Mother]

During the months of the protest some people of the Protestant faith expressed their views. The following extract from a six-page letter is a flavour of what was said:

Holy Cross School has received letters of support from all over the world. I also think it is dreadful that these dear little children are subjected to all of this bitterness and hatred. This comes from the residents (apparently) and also from the parents and friends of the children and of course yourself as well.

As a Protestant, but first and more importantly as a Christian, I have been blessed and privileged by meeting, praying and praising our God and Saviour Jesus Christ with wonderful Christian Catholics.

I assumed Roman Catholic Priests were Christian men and teach 'their people' about the love of Jesus Christ but seeing how you are dealing with the situation in Ardoyne, it makes me wonder. Do you only wear the cross on your clothing, around your neck or in your heart?

I only write to admonish you another Christian (assuming that is what you are) […] It seems to me that you have aggravated the situation and also have created a lot of bitterness throughout our land wedging a deeper division between our two communities […] You and 'your people' have managed to blacken the Protestant people of Northern Ireland throughout the world (this is only possible because people are so willing to believe a lie) […]

I will also pray for you Father Troy that God will open your eyes and heart to the truth and you will see what is happening here.

P.S. I am sorry because of some of the terrible happenings in our country; I am unable to give you my address.

Criticism for speaking to the media came on headed notepaper from a group in Dublin:

We are the participants on the [...] course at [...] in Dublin. We feel that your over enthusiasm to engage with the media is only serving to further polarise an already divided community.

The way I dressed as well as my presence there was criticised:

I feel moved to write this note to you as I was uncomfortable seeing you on television walking on Ardoyne Road wearing your 'badge of office' – Cross and Passion. I am discomforted with *any* Church involvement in protests or walks.

One letter arriving in those days spoke in a moving way of what life in Glenbryn had been like:

When I was first married 50 years ago my husband and I went to live in Glenbryn Park. The people were so good to me. I was the only Catholic at the top of the Street. They all helped me to look after our daughter and let my husband and I get to Church. I could never forget them.

In truth, the overwhelming number of letters and messages received were of a most encouraging and positive nature. Some were words of personal encouragement and support. The following arrived from someone in County Fermanagh:

Those on either side of the street abusing the parents and children going to your school have been called Protestants. I, by my home background, schooling and church membership would be described as Protestant. But, I am thoroughly ashamed at the behaviour of my co-religionists, and am writing to express my sorrow at, and apologies for their actions. And I know of many other Protestants who share my revulsion and shame at what is happening.

A letter from County Galway contained eight pages of signatures:

We the undersigned clergy, parishioners, teachers and pupils of the Church of Ireland parish of [...] in [...] support the right of your parishioners – the children and parents of those attending Holy Cross Primary School in Ardoyne – to travel to and from school, through its main entrance, in an atmosphere of respect, dignity and peace.

At our service this morning, we prayed that God would sustain you all through your awful present distress.

However, in spite of this great support, it was clear that people had become tired of stories coming out of Northern of Ireland. The following, from a 'Christian Group, Scotland', may be extreme but may reflect tiredness on the part of people:

Sir,

Anyone with half a brain can see peace will never come to Northern Ireland [...] My idea would be to bulldoze the whole area. Then the small minded would have nothing to riot about.

Some people had practical suggestions such as the following from County Clare:

If the children stopped going to school for about a month things would settle down and it would be better than having someone killed or injured, even the RUC.

Each day brought extraordinary letters and messages. Clergy and religious communities throughout Ireland and further away expressed their solidarity and support. People of all denominations made contact and the overwhelming majority expressed care and worry for the safety of the children and the health of the parents. The school and its teachers were mentioned in most letters with special admiration for its principal, Anne Tanney.

No matter to what sector a person belongs, the opinions and sentiments of your colleagues are important. The National Conference of Priests wrote in a most positive way to Fr Gary and me. Further, they went to the bother of sending a representative to Holy Cross to express the solidarity of this group. Passionists from other communities visited us and phoned. In particular, Fr Brian D'Arcy CP visited most Fridays.

Modern communications ensured that a great number of messages arrived by email. My efforts to keep up with all of this correspondence did not see many answered for some considerable time.

On a personal note, I will never forget my birthday of 2001. Because of a meeting attempting to end the protest I was not on the road as the parents went to collect the children one afternoon in early October. Fr Gary let people know that my birthday was on 9 October. I knew nothing about this and was totally surprised and delighted when I arrived on the road that morning to be met with cards, presents, singing of 'Happy Birthday' and good wishes. Some of this was captured by media present. I have kept all those cards and will always treasure them as a reminder of how thoughtful people can be amidst their own sufferings.

The search for a way out of the unfolding tragedy never ceased. Driven by the visible deterioration of the children (though the school and the various services provided were of the highest order), politicians, community workers, trade unionists, churches and individuals made many sincere and creative efforts to find a solution.

There were also many people who prayed and fasted for us and who became a source of enormous strength in those days. In 1992, I had given up smoking with great difficulty. Never was I more tempted to begin again than during those awful days of protest. I thank God that I didn't start again! People with great faith in a particular picture or devotion sent material to us in the hope that an end might come to the suffering of the children. Members of the Maranatha Community came to visit Holy Cross regularly on their visits from England and prayed constantly for us.

A most helpful suggestion came from a person who was in regular contact and who was qualified in law. It was to consider taking a court action to challenge the way the protest was being treated by politicians and how it was being policed. There was no doubt in the minds of many people that the health and safety of the children were being sacrificed in order to prevent outbreaks of violence elsewhere. In other words, had the rights of the child been upheld, the consequences would have demanded wholesale arrests and an end to the protest.

The person making the suggestion strongly encouraged me to consider taking such a course of action. Anything was worth trying if it had even a slight chance of getting the children out of the terrifying daily abuse. I got a few details from this person and shortly afterwards made it publically known.

The reaction was immediate. There was great interest in what I had in mind and when it would begin, who would pay for it, who would take the action, what I hoped to achieve and many other questions. There was concern, for example, that if such a court action, even if taken at once, failed, the children and their parents might be left in a more dangerous situation.

To protect the anonymity of the person suggesting this course of action, I had to do my best to answer the questions as they were posed. In the evening, I could find out more from my contact and have enough information to give some answers.

Personally, I had no interest in spending time in the courts, but we were running out of options. In any event, the protest was suspended before an action could be taken.

Visits to the Northern Ireland Office and to the office of First and Deputy First Ministers were always conducted in a most courteous and polite fashion. It became clear to me that there was a desire to end the protest but that the means to be used had to be politically correct. The sense of urgency of getting the children out of this highly damaging and dangerous situation never seemed to be there.

Had I been the father or grandfather of a child walking to and from school each day, it might be that ties to my child would have created a desperate urgency to see the whole thing ended. These children were not connected to me by blood relationship but their pain was most definitely mine. Their tears became mine and their fear broke my heart.

I have to confess to losing my patience in a serious way during one meeting between officials from the office of the First and Deputy First Minister and the Board of Governors.

Everyone present came to that meeting in Holy Cross Monastery in total good faith and with a wish to be helpful. The longer the meeting went on, however, the clearer it became to the governors that we were being asked to accept that the underlying issues needing attention in North Belfast would have to be resolved first if the school

With Anne Tanney, Principal of Holy Cross Girls' School

With Fr Gary during the protest in 2001

Anne Tanney with some of the pupils

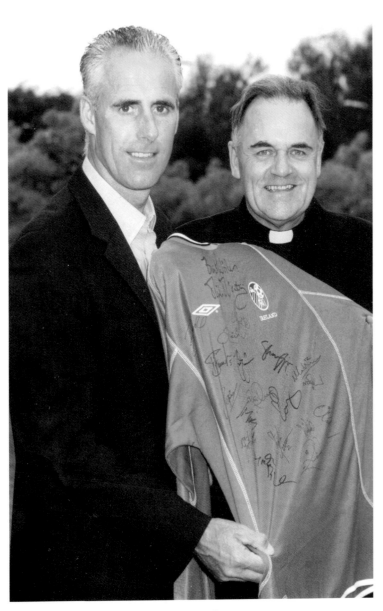

*Mick McCarthy, then Irish soccer manager,
presents a signed jersey as an auction item for Holy Cross*

Ss John and Paul's Monastery, Rome,
where I was stationed from 1994 until 2001

My father, Dan Troy, who died on 27 October 2001

With Cardinal Ratzinger, later Pope Benedict XVI,
at Regenburg Passionist Monastery, Bavaria, August 1995

With Pope John Paul II in 1994

protest were to end. It was not put as bluntly as that, but that was the suggestion.

With more forceful language and more emotion than needed, I 'exploded'. From the moment of my arrival in Ardoyne, I had accepted and publicly acknowledged that the issues of the protestors must be my issues also if wounds were to be healed. As previously stated, what I could never accept was that children, of any religion or none, could be kept in danger as some sort of bargaining chip.

That particular meeting ended without much progress being made. I was shocked that the officials were comfortable talking about the issues needing attention taking months to advance to a point where a resolution of the protest might be brought about. For me, another day was a day too long. When further meetings took place with those officials and with the First and Deputy First Minister, a sense of urgency about getting the children out of danger gradually emerged.

Dialogue is essential as an alternative to violence. Unknown to the parents, I was approached one morning by a lady who had some startling information. Through contacts in the Republic of Ireland, she had been approached by a group of people preparing to come to Belfast to sort out the protest in its own way. The intention of those in the group was to attack the homes of the protestors during the night. The number in the group coming together was in hundreds and these people would be prepared to fight to end the protest and in their view render the children safe.

The group was ready to put its plan into action as soon as the word was given. This absolutely shocked and terrified me. My nightmare all along was that someone would be killed.

The group concerned was not a paramilitary group or in any way connected to one. The Good Friday Agreement, the ceasefires and all the efforts for peace and reconciliation would have been dealt a severe if not a fatal blow if this attack had happened. The restraint and dignity of the parents and children had been so great and without a trace of retaliation. Now, we faced what was a well-intentioned act of support that could have led to bloodshed and, quite possibly, death. If such an attack took place, the consequences would be horrendous.

Immediately, with the help of this lady, the group was contacted and a plan put in place to ensure that no such action would be taken. Many hours were spent by this woman persuading the group that its actions would put the children in deadly danger. Eventually, I got word that the plan had been cancelled and no attack would take place. I thanked the intermediary and God that a serious tragedy had been averted.

When I met with An Taoiseach on 17 October 2001 at Government Buildings, I made him aware of this matter as part of our conversation. To ensure that no life was put in danger anywhere in Ardoyne, the local police were made aware that such a threat had existed.

An incident such as this showed me how dangerous our situation had become. People were becoming intolerant of what was happening to the children. A message from England at this time described my attitude as 'complacent', but personal criticism was the least of my worries during those days. The one principle that guided me was not to say or do anything that would escalate the situation.

There was no easy way out. Some days, the protest was low key and it became noticeable that the morning protestors were normally fewer in number than those in the afternoons, but, the longer the protest continued, the greater the danger that it would last a long time and it was becoming clear that even a few protestors would keep Ardoyne Road closed to the children.

CHAPTER SEVEN

THE FIRST BLESSING of the Book of Genesis upon our first parents is to be fruitful and multiply and to fill the earth. Numerous children would be seen as a sign of blessing and of God's favour. We priests of the Roman family of the faith are not called to share in this particular blessing. Whether we should be or not is a question for another time and another place. However, God blessed me late in life with not just one special child or even a few chosen children. It was my blessing to inherit 225 of the most wonderful children anyone could ever wish to know and love. On 3 September 2001, by extraordinary circumstances, I discovered something of what it is like to take your child to school for the first time. What a tragedy it turned out to be for the little ones who had so looked forward to that morning.

By the middle of October, many avenues to seek a solution had been pursued by different people. On a personal level, I never lost my sense of outrage at what was happening to innocent children. Parent meetings were held regularly to make sure that as many parents as possible had their voice heard. Some of these meetings were stormy, and who could blame a father or mother for expressing disgust at what was happening?

A meeting between Glenbryn residents and Ardoyne community representatives was held on 9 October. One of the Ardoyne representatives was also a school governor. Two others had children at Holy Cross Girls' School. The six Ardoyne representatives at all times made it clear to the six Glenbryn delegates that dialogue and the setting up of a community forum would be discussed only when the protest was lifted. For their part, the Glenbryn delegates insisted that if the protest were to be suspended or called off, they would require some sort of reciprocation. The Ardoyne delegation saw reciprocation as being the setting up of a community forum at which all issues concerning both communities could be discussed and representatives of the parents committee (RTE group) would take part. Ideas were presented for consideration by both parties and by the wider communities they represented. Only dialogue and breaking down mistrust would lead us out of the horror of the protest to some form of living in peace.

Towards the end of the meeting the urgency of immediately stopping the protest was impressed on the Glenbryn representatives. Following this meeting consultation was due to take place with the wider Glenbryn community.

In drawing the meeting to a close, the Ardoyne representatives stated that the next point of contact should be with Billy Hutchinson (Progressive Unionist) who would then in turn contact Gerry Kelly (Sinn Féin).

The wish of the Glenbryn community to have a new peace wall across Ardoyne Road surfaced again at this time. The North Belfast MP, Nigel Dodds, asked the British government to reconsider its decision not to erect a security gate across Ardoyne Road. On 10 October, Northern Ireland Security Minister Jane Kennedy had ordered the building of a new peace line to separate loyalist Glenbryn and nationalist Alliance Avenue, which back onto each other. Nigel Dodds saw the job as being left half done unless the problems of the Ardoyne Road itself were addressed. However, the minister rejected requests for a permanent security gate to be built on the Ardoyne Road.

Progressive Unionist Assembly Member Billy Hutchinson said that Jane Kennedy did not understand that loyalist residents wanted a gate erected which would be shut only at night, to prevent attacks on Glenbryn. He is quoted as saying 'The woman does not understand the problems of Northern Ireland, she should resign and go back to Liverpool.' (Ms Kennedy represented the Liverpool Wavertree constituency).

In fact, the minister did understand very clearly the issue regarding a gate across Ardoyne Road. This proposal had surfaced in the 1990s and would surface again. The unacceptability of the locked gate across Ardoyne Road was put to the minister by the Holy Cross School governors in a clear and definite way. It was not that the Ardoyne people wanted to prevent the residents of Glenbryn from feeling safer in their homes, but simply that the day the gate was built, Holy Cross Girls' Primary School would be forced to close.

With trust at zero, no parents would feel safe with their children in school and the possibility that the gate could be locked at any stage, thus denying them access to the school. There was also the fear that the key to the gate could become a source of control and power over the parents and the children. If the gate could not be opened any morning, the school could not open either.

In a situation where there was a modicum of trust, there would be no need for a gate. In the absence of such trust, a gate would be neither acceptable nor effective.

On 10 October, Bishop James Simon Jefery, an Anglo-Catholic bishop from Hampshire, England, arrived in Ardoyne to see if he could help to bring about a resolution. Laura McDonald, the administrator who accompanied the bishop, wrote up a seven-page account of the visit. At the invitation of the parents, Bishop Jefery walked up the road with the parents as they went to the school to collect their children. He described the walk as 'quite eerie'. On arrival at the school, he was 'shell-shocked' and added that 'Our United Kingdom was very much disunited. It was more like civil war.'

Turning to his faith, he said 'I couldn't help but think of the strange similarity of this road to Calvary – and the betrayal by their own kind.' The report ends with 'There can be no Peace which is not founded on Justice first.'

In a letter forwarding the report to me, Bishop Jefery wrote that the 'report will be on the Prime Minister's desk so that he is in no doubt about the true situation at Holy Cross School.' One assumes that Prime Minister Blair received the report, but there was no response from him. The report indicated that it was also being copied to the House of Commons and House of Lords as well as the Primate of All Ireland, Archbishop Seán Brady.

Bishop Jefery kept in constant contact and paid a number of visits to Holy Cross. His interest and support were greatly appreciated by all he met on the road and in the school. He wished to see the good relations re-established between Wheatfield and Holy Cross schools.

Meanwhile, efforts by the Stormont administration continued, to try to find a way out. A memo aimed at bringing representatives from Ardoyne and Glenbryn together was distributed on 17 October. The plan was to have the meeting on Wednesday, 24 October, or soon after. A note of hope was struck when the memo said:

> It is anticipated that during the process of preparation the protest will be suspended pending the outcome of the discussions. It is also anticipated that parents would have the choice of how they get the children to school and home again, but would be encouraged to use a variety of transport methods and routes.

Alas, the suspension of the protest never materialised.

Meetings with neighbouring Protestant clergy were also a source of help and encouragement. Their options were limited and they could not deliver a whole community who passionately believed in the rightness of their case or the legitimacy of the protest. It was not an easy situation for them and each had to decide how best to act in the light of their overall situation.

On 16 October, the school governors were greatly helped by a talk by a Belfast solicitor of great experience. His aim was to help us to see how a legal action to end the protest by means of the courts might be pursued. He outlined a number of options but added that it was not possible to guarantee that any of the options would prove successful. It was decided that we could keep court action as a possibility while pursuing the road of dialogue as best we could.

This meeting was held in the seventh week of the protest. It was heartbreaking to hear that thirty-four pupils had been identified as suffering from serious trauma. Of these, fifteen children, with the agreement of their parents, had been referred to a professional counselling service.

Two days later, the Committee on the Administration of Justice

(CAJ) forwarded to the school governors copies of letters they had sent to the Chief Constable and to the Minister of Education about their responsibilities under international human rights law to protect the 'best interests' of the child.

At a Geneva meeting on UK government compliance with human rights standards, CAJ got some United Nations Committee members to ask questions of the British Government delegation about the situation in Ardoyne. While this did not alter the situation on the ground, it was another forum at which the plight of the children could be examined.

On Friday morning, 19 October, the Board of Governors met in Holy Cross Girls' School with representatives from Glenbryn. This meeting had been difficult to arrange. Some of the parents felt that it was not right that people from the community who had protested against their children should be allowed into the school. In order to break down a barrier, the school governors held out for the meeting being held in the school. This was a sign of some little progress. For the Glenbryn representatives, too, it was a decision not easily taken. Tribute must be paid to these people for coming to the meeting in the school.

The previous weekend had been a difficult one with intense violence on the streets. It is important to remember that education does not take place in a vacuum and so what was happening on the streets and in the locality also affected the children of all schools returning to school after the weekend. The level of fear, lack of sleep, and the widening of the gap within the community were all augmented by violence on the streets.

In the previous week, meetings had been held with the office of First Minister and Deputy First Minister at Stormont, with RUC senior officers, and with Jane Kennedy, Security Minister in the Northern Ireland Office. However, as we sat with the Glenbryn representatives there was little light at the end of a very dark tunnel.

On 27 September, Jane Kennedy had called for the ending of the school protest. In the light of the judicial review taken by one of the parents against the NIO and the police, it is interesting to read what she said:

There can be no acceptable level of harassment and intimidation of children.

The world's press may have gone but threatening and abusive behaviour goes on and to continue to subject primary school children to it is outrageous.

[Press Office, Castle Buildings, Stormont, Belfast]

It was interesting to hear in court counsel for the NIO avoiding any admissions such as that quoted above.

One thing that both sides of the meeting agreed upon was that the situation in the wider context of North Belfast was deteriorating. We could all see that the Holy Cross protest contributed to this and was in turn fuelled by wider issues.

Anne Tanney, the school principal, expressed the grave concern that she and others had about the long-term effects the situation would have on the children, and highlighted how the school had worked extremely hard over the previous thirty years to build and maintain good community relations with the residents in the area.

The representatives of Glenbryn asked the school governors if we could provide any suggestions which might assist with moving the situation forward in relation to the protest. This showed just how far we were from a solution: the governors had only one proposal on the table and that was to end the protest and immediately begin to address the issues presented by the residents of Glenbryn.

There had been reports in the press that the protest could be ended if the school would agree to what the residents were asking. The Glenbryn representatives clarified for us that, following the trouble that had arisen on 19 June, they did not want the children to be brought to and from school in cars. They proposed the use of Belfast Education and Library Board buses to transport the pupils, and they assured us that they would view these buses as coming from a neutral source. Parents would be able to accompany their children on the two-way journey.

The Glenbryn residents believed that this would help diffuse the situation and create the right conditions to move forward. However, we believed that, as governors, we could not dictate to parents how their children go to and from school. Over the previous thirty years, pupils had walked or cycled to school or travelled by bus, car or taxi. Now the sole means of getting there would be buses provided by the local education board. To meet a temporary situation, we might have felt able to recommend to the parents such a choice, but this proposal was a final solution and, once implemented, it would be difficult to alter it. Even after such a short time in Ardoyne, I knew that the proposal stood no chance of getting parental approval.

We asked the resident representatives if they could include walking as an option, as well as using buses. Our argument was that if that arrangement helped to diffuse tensions in the area, the issue of cars taking children to school could be looked at in a more peaceful context. It saddened me that often I was accused of being party to the abuse of the Holy Cross children by not promoting the option of accepting buses as the sole means of getting to school. But it would not be acceptable for school children in Dublin or London or anywhere else to be taken to school not as their parents chose, but as their neighbours dictated.

It was following this meeting that I pointed out that the only place on earth where little girls were denied an education was Afghanistan. The day after I made this comment, there were placards held up by the protestors saying: 'Fr Troy: Girls in Afghanistan go to school by bus.' There was still some humour left in an otherwise tense situation.

During the meeting, the Glenbryn group raised the vexed issue of the use – by parents and others – of video cameras to film protesters on Ardoyne Road. This continued to be an issue until the suspension of the protest. Some of the international observers were upset when, early on in the protest, I asked them not to use cameras. I received a rather stern letter about this matter, pointing out how wrong I was to take this stance. It was not that I did not see the value of collecting evidence of what was happening, but my concern was that the anger of the protestors might add to the suffering of the children on the next school journey. Looking back, I feel I should have kept out of this issue of the cameras.

There is every reason to believe that a video camera was being used from an upstairs bedroom window of a house on Ardoyne Road to capture the walk of the children and parents. Also, the RUC frequently filmed the children and parents as they came past the military vehicles that blocked our way each day. It remains a mystery why the children and parents should have been so frequently filmed by the police. Had we committed crimes or trespassed on Ardoyne Road, I could understand the need to collect evidence. But we were bringing children to and from school, and it is amazing that this legitimate activity was being videoed. Without doubt, this added to the trauma inflicted on the children. When I asked the police about this, I never got a satisfactory answer. Their 'operational reasons' explanation seemed to cover a multitude.

Another issue raised with us by the Glenbryn residents was that, on occasion, a number of pupils from a neighbouring Catholic school were seen accompanying the parents coming down the road. It was clear to us that no parent or guardian would deliberately put a child in danger by walking them through this highly dangerous protest. However, sometimes children collected from different schools will end up walking home under the care of the one adult, and this was the simple explanation in this case.

There is, however, an underlying issue of ownership regarding who can and cannot walk 'our' road and also when and in what company they can do this. If the children of Holy Cross were not still in such acute danger, this issue could have been raised at the meeting. But we did not want to make the situation worse for the children the next day.

The question of acceptability of people in some areas continues, as I was to learn. As chairperson of the Board of Governors of St Gabriel's College, Crumlin Road, I was asked by the principal to attend an event in a school in a strongly loyalist area. The two schools had co-operated over a number of years on various projects, and still do. The Secretary of State, Dr. John Reid, was to attend a ceremony at that school to mark this co-operation. When the principal of St Gabriel's sent the list of guests to the other school, there was an objection raised to my name being on it. It was said that if I did attend, there would be a protest outside the school to object to my presence in a school in that area. To my great disappointment, I was asked by the principal of St

Gabriel's not to join other school governors and teachers at the event. I can only presume that my role in the Holy Cross protest made me unacceptable in 'their' area.

I had no option but to stand down lest I should be the cause of suffering at the school concerned. On hearing that I was not welcome in the school, I sent a fax to Dr Reid, asking him to address the issue the following day, when he met with teachers and governors from both schools. I received no acknowledgement to this message. The principal of St Gabriel's College did raise the issue with the Secretary of State, but no satisfactory response was forthcoming. That the children of this school were not subjected to a protest pleased me greatly. That people responsible for the education of young people gave in to such threats worried me then and worries me now.

Another contentious issue raised by the Glenbryn residents was that more people came back down the road than went up with the children. The worry of the residents was that people other than parents were joining the walk with the children. There is no denying that sometimes there were people who were not parents or guardians walking with the children on their way home from school. However, it was difficult to prevent genuinely concerned people from accompanying a grandchild, a niece or other relative. On occasion, to try to respond to this concern of the residents, I did try asking that only parents or guardians walk the road. Relatives and some others pointed out to me that I had no right to interfere with their right to walk on Ardoyne Road. Some did accept, however, that for the sake of the children, they would not walk with them.

The Glenbryn residents brought to our attention two specific statements made to the press which were perceived as unhelpful. The school had no official spokesperson, and Anne Tanney and I were the main speakers. However, we soon learned that, although we always tried to speak in a spirit of peace and reconciliation, once we spoke, we had no further control over how the words were presented or what headlines were used. We made it clear to the Glenbryn delegation that we would retain the right to continue issuing statements as we felt either necessary or helpful.

This meeting ended with both parties agreeing that we were

working towards the same fundamental aim of securing an end to the protest. While the meeting clearly did not bring a solution, we saw it as a positive step.

The day before the meeting, I had been invited to visit President Mary McAleese at Áras an Uachtaráin and then to go to Government Buildings to meet with An Taoiseach Bertie Ahern. From previous contact, I knew that both wanted nothing more than a resolution to the protest, and this for the sake of all concerned. At this stage, I was beginning to wonder if the children could take much more of the daily strain, so all such meetings were of the utmost importance.

At Áras an Uachtaráin I was welcomed with the warmth and kindness I had experienced on previous visits, and I found it encouraging to meet with as wise and experienced a person as President McAleese. She had also been a parishioner of Holy Cross, and proud to be such – *From Ardoyne to the Áras* is the title of a biography recently published – and she knew Holy Cross Primary School at first-hand. As President of Ireland, she was not in a position to make a public statement on our talks. However, I was free to say what took place and did so.

The President expressed her outrage that this abuse of small children was dragging on for two months of the current school term. She likened it to a form of terrorism being daily directed at children going to school and said that it would also affect children of other schools who witnessed the events. As a lawyer, she maintained that no protest is lawful that employs the use of bombs, bottles, balloons of urine and the like. She asked to be kept informed of developments and told me that she was praying for all, including the Glenbryn community, that this chapter of our history would soon be over.

I was grateful to her, her husband and staff for the welcome and encouragement given by this visit. It was strange in many ways to walk back to the car park and realise that the President of Ireland was so compassionate and sought only the reconciliation that would prevent anything like this ever happening again to any child.

From the Phoenix Park where the President resides to Government Buildings in Merrion Street is not far as the crow flies, but Dublin traffic can make it seem like a great distance. An Taoiseach gave an hour of his time to discuss how the children could be taken out of this situation. He was remarkably well informed. Through the British-Irish Secretariat and through government officials who visited Holy Cross regularly, he had kept up-to-date with what was happening. He also had reports from discussions held with loyalists, some of whom supported the protest at Holy Cross.

During that hour of discussion, it was clear to me that Bertie Ahern was deeply moved by what was happening daily on Ardoyne Road. Like anyone who knew anything of the suffering that was being inflicted on the children, he wished to explore every avenue to end it all. Also, he was concerned for the protestors and wished that they could be helped to find a way of ending such negative worldwide publicity.

The following press release was issued by the Department of An Taoiseach on completion of our discussions.

An Taoiseach, Mr Bertie Ahern, T.D., met today with Fr Aidan Troy, parish priest of Ardoyne and chair of the Board of Governors of Holy Cross Girls Primary School.

The Taoiseach welcomed the opportunity to hear from Fr Troy about the current difficulties in Ardoyne and, in particular, the harm which is being done to the young children by the ongoing protests outside their school.

Speaking after the meeting, the Taoiseach said:

> The children of Holy Cross School have been subjected to appalling treatment during the course of the protests. While the Glenbryn and Ardoyne communities may have serious problems to address, there can be no justification for a protest targeted at young children. The protest at the school should be brought to an end immediately, before more damage is inflicted on the innocent victims of this dispute.
>
> I also want to condemn in the strongest possible terms yesterday's blast-bomb attack on Alliance Avenue which terrified the children at Holy Cross as they were walking home from school.
>
> I understand that efforts are being made to address

the wider concerns of the two communities in Ardoyne and Glenbryn and I welcome such initiatives.

I would also urge local politicians and community representatives to re-double their efforts in the coming days to facilitate inter-community dialogue and local agreement on the way forward.

Only by talking and working together can the two communities resolve their differences and build a decent future for their children.' [18 October 2001]

One other issue caused me great concern at the time, and that was my father's health. He had worked all his life on the railway. As a passenger guard, he had worked particularly on trains to the west of Ireland. A most outgoing man who loved company, he was also a good golfer and very proud to be a member of Woodbrook Artisans' Golf Association, outside Bray, where he lived all his life. He was immensely proud of his family, not least my brother, Philip, the eldest, his wife, Mary, and their two children, Ciarán and Sinéad.

Since the death of our mother, my father had lived with my sister, Helen. When she moved house, he went along and was the cook of the household. An easygoing man, he seldom complained about any aches or pains, which may have been through a fear of having to go into hospital. In March 2001, he and Helen had visited me in Rome as they did regularly while I lived there. During that visit, on St. Patrick's Day he complained of being very cold and was unwell for the rest of his time in Rome. His journey home was difficult and Helen wondered if he would survive it. He did and gradually got back to something of his previous form. However, when I got home from Rome in July I could see that he was not his usual self. Once I got to Ardoyne, my visits to see him in Bray were less frequent than they might have been. When I did see him over that summer, I could see that he was not well and was nervous about his own health. He had given up smoking at the age of 83 years and was now 87.

It became clear that he needed medical attention and he was admitted to Loughlinstown Hospital in south Dublin. Apart from a brief stay in hospital many years before, when he had been knocked off his bicycle, this was a new experience for him. As often as I could, I would call to see him and always found him in good form if somewhat quieter than usual. Other family members kept me in touch with his progress. The care and attention of all in the hospital was superb. They were preparing him for heart surgery and were confident that he would come through it well.

As the end of October approached, everyone was looking forward to the midterm break at Halloween. The children of the area were looking forward to 'trick or treat', and many of the homes were decorated with witches, broomsticks, pumpkins and other such items. The teachers and school staff were drained and needed to get away from the daily pressures, not alone of their regular tasks but also of never knowing whether they would get to and from school without incident. Fr Gary and I had talked about how each of us would take some time off to get a break and be back in time for the return to school at the beginning of November.

The plea of the parents after the two months since the school reopened was summed up by one who said, 'Please leave our children alone.' Another mother who had made her way to school every day since 3 September summed up the experience as follows:

Every Monday is just like the first day all over again. Every Monday feels like the third of September. When you wake up every day you feel dread but Mondays are the worst because you have the weekend to unwind and then you realise you have a whole week of the protest ahead.

[*Irish News,* 30 October 2001 p.18]

On the same page, the residents' viewpoint was given by a community leader. He felt that the people of Glenbryn had been subjected to intimidation and acts of violence. Criticism was made of parents bringing their children to school along Ardoyne Road and through the protest. The conclusion offered was that the children were being used as political pawns. The protestors must also have looked forward to a break from standing on the road six times each day.

The police were facing the changeover from RUC to Police Service of Northern Ireland (PSNI) before we returned to school on

Monday, 5 November, but it was clear that, short of a miracle, we would all be back in place as the school reopened. There would be meetings needed with police to arrange for security matters, such as ensuring the safety of the school grounds and the road to the school, but for now, we were all looking forward to a few days off. So, when the school closed on Friday, 26 October, it was to the enormous relief of everyone.

I planned to travel to London on Saturday 27 October, to visit a family where I could rest for a few days. I was so looking forward to this break. But God had other plans.

On Friday night, as I was going to bed, my sister phoned to say that she had been called to the hospital earlier in the evening as my father's condition had altered. After some time he seemed to recover sufficiently for the medical and nursing staff to advise her to return home. She was content that he was comfortable for the night and saw no reason why I should not go ahead with my plans to travel to London the following day.

At 1.30 a.m., the phone beside my bed rang. It was my sister to say that our father had just died. She was in the hospital. My brother came on the phone and suggested that I could wait until the morning before travelling to Bray, but I knew that I would leave immediately.

Above all nights to do so, I had gone to bed with very little petrol in the car, but before getting to the M1, I found an all-night garage and filled up for the sad journey ahead. When I got to Dublin at about 4 a.m., I was driving down Gardiner Street in the heart of the city when I came up behind a car driving very slowly. After I had overtaken it, the car sped up, overtook me and waved me to the side of the road. It was an unmarked Garda car and I had broken the speed limit. This was not something I needed at that hour of the morning 4 a.m. as I made my way to see my dead father.

It was over 37 years since my mother's death. The intervening years had been blessed in that my father enjoyed a happy and good life. Now his family and a huge range of people came to bury him. About two years before he died, my father let it be known that, when he died, his wish was to be cremated. This surprised us but he was quite clear that this was his wish.

The day of the funeral in Bray was a very sad occasion but the support of so many people helped greatly. One very moving moment for me was when I saw a group of parents and school governors from Holy Cross in the church for the funeral Mass. It turned out that a bus had been hired and, with an early start, had reached Bray to offer support and sympathy. Most of these people I had known for only the two months since the school had reopened. Fr Gary, other Passionist colleagues and other clergy were of great support during the funeral Mass.

Because of the situation since my arrival in Holy Cross I knew that I had not spent as much time as I would have liked with my father in his final illness. The greatest consolation for me came when I was told how proud my father was of his family and of my work in Belfast.

The funeral over, I was able to prepare to return to Holy Cross and get ready for the return to school on 5 November. It was almost as if my father had died at a time that would be most convenient in the events that had unfolded in Ardoyne.

On my return, I found that the children had a good break for Halloween and were looking forward to getting back to school, meeting their friends and being back with their teachers, but there was great concern about what would happen on Ardoyne Road on Monday morning.

I was concerned that I had not been able to arrange a meeting with the police when I got back from the funeral in Bray. It was difficult for them to contact me while I was away. Eventually I got a call late on Sunday evening to say that Assistant Chief Constable Alan McQuillan and District Commander Roger Maxwell would call to Holy Cross. They arrived shortly after 10.30 p.m. to let me know of their assessment for the return to school the next morning.

Much to my surprise, they told me that following talks with the residents of Glenbryn, there would be a change in their approach to policing on Ardoyne Road the next morning. The police (now the PSNI) would be wearing yellow coats and no balaclavas or boiler suits, and would be carrying no shields or batons. In truth, no one could do other than welcome such a softening of the approach.

However, I knew that this would pose a problem for the parents once they arrived at the military vehicles blocking Ardoyne Road. The suddenness of the change and the total lack of consultation with them would cause anger, surprise and alarm. After all, it was the children who were being targeted but the consultation and subsequent agreement had been solely with the perpetrators of the blockade.

When this point of consulting and informing the parents was raised at a later date, the response from the PSNI was that I, as chair of governors of the school, knew in advance. While this was technically true, information received an hour before midnight on Sunday night hardly qualified as adequate notice.

My worst fears came true as the parents and children arrived on Ardoyne Road on Monday morning. The reduction in the number of police and military vehicles lining each side of the road was a concern for the parents. In normal circumstances, any right-thinking person would welcome this reduction, but where trust is absent, things are seen differently. There were also questions asked of me as to whether I had agreed to this new arrangement and why the opinion of the parents had not been sought. Some of the parents did not know that I had been away at my father's funeral for most of the previous week.

Over the Halloween break, extensive discussions had taken place with elected, community and statutory representatives. These discussions were with an interdepartmental group which included people from the devolved Administration as well as the Northern Ireland Office and a senior liaison officer from the Office of the First and Deputy First Minister. The aim of these discussions was to consider measures which might be put in place to tackle the complex community issues in the Glenbryn area and which could be applied to other areas of North Belfast.

The report of the senior liaison officer on 1 November 2001, while schools were closed, affirms that work had already begun on the Alliance Avenue/Glenbryn Peace Wall. Police resources on a 24-hour-a-day basis were promised. Measures were being actively pursued to protect windows on houses in Glenbryn close to the interface with Ardoyne. Work to address housing needs in Glenbryn was seen as a high priority for the Northern Ireland Housing Executive. The Training and Employment Agency was to deliver outreach and awareness sessions for Glenbryn/Ardoyne residents. There was a call for community dialogue and the development of community infrastructure which could contribute to the creation of vibrant and stable communities. An independent Action Research Project was proposed – this was to identify goals, priorities and strategic activities aimed at building community capacity. And there were also ideas sought that would help regenerate the environmental interface between Glenbryn and Ardoyne. It was recognised that this would require cross-community support and active community involvement.

Nobody could deny the good intentions of those seeking to implement the matters raised above. Of course, every community must be able to live in peace and without threat. My difficulty was that it would take time even to get agreement on these matters, and it was not right that children should have to wait.

So, on this first day back, it was with real fear in their hearts and great concern for the walk to school that parents awaited clearance to proceed towards the school. The police uniforms had changed but little else had. The protestors were there to 'welcome' us back to school, with the familiar taunting, abusive language and whistles. It is interesting that after the break of a week, it was a shock to have to walk through such a hostile group of people.

At the invitation of the Right to Education group, Mary Banotti, MEP, accompanied the parents and their children from the top of Alliance Avenue to the school. She wrote a detailed report which she sent to President McAleese, An Taoiseach, Bertie Ahern, and to a number of TDs and senators as well as to David Trimble.

In her report she writes:

Never in my political life have I witnessed such an intimidating, and in my opinion, illegal and unlawful situation.

I spoke to the senior police officers who assured me that they were doing their best to come to some sort of an accommodation. However, I believe that what is going on, on that road, is both illegal, intimidatory and totally unacceptable at this stage in the history of Northern Ireland [...]

It is my opinion that these children are being denied their basic human rights and under the UN Declaration of the Rights of the Child these children are entitled to have an education and to access that education without fear or intimidation.

[Report on visit of Mary Banotti MEP on Monday 5 November 2001]

David Trimble, writing on 9 November 2001, thanks Mary Banotti for her report but raises a number of issues:

- Omitted from the report that 'the gross intimidation of school children is only a symptom of a much deeper and profound problem in the Ardoyne area'.

- Although there is orchestration of the situation by paramilitary elements on both sides, there are genuine grievances on the Protestant side – as well as the very obvious grievance on the Catholic side – which you make no mention of in your report.

- It is unfortunate that members of the security forces here, unlike the Republic, have to be armed but that is a direct consequence of the threat they are under from armed groups, loyalist and republican.

- I note too that when the police adopted a more 'softline' approach this week in response to de-escalation of the protest, there were complaints from the Right to Education Group. There is clearly a propagandist element at work here.

- It sends out the wrong signal when politicians from the Republic berate members of our police service as if, somehow, they were the guilty party. I believe that the police response in a very provocative situation has been restrained and professional.

- The right to education is inalienable in a western democracy. So too is the right to assemble in peace and to protest peaceably.

- I believe that it is only when politicians from the Republic are informed as to the causes – as well as the effects – of the protest in Ardoyne that a proper understanding of this horrible situation will be arrived at.

I found it interesting that Mary Banotti came in her role as a Member of the European Parliament. Since my arrival in Belfast a few months earlier, following seven years living in Italy, I had noticed the absence of any regular references to our membership of the European Union.

Mary Banotti kept in regular contact and arranged for her sister, Fine Gael TD, Nora Owen, to ask the Minister for Foreign Affairs about the efforts he had made to have the situation resolved and to make a statement on the matter. A written answer was received from the then Minister, Brian Cowen TD.

With the new police arrangements, the footpath on which we had not been able to walk since 3 September was free of security force vehicles as we neared the school gates. On reaching this part of the road, some parents moved on to the footpath for the last few paces to the school gates. Some of the protestors, on seeing this, expressed their disapproval to the police. Immediately a police officer physically tried to remove a father who was holding the hand of his daughter. The child went hysterical as the father resisted and was being pushed off the footpath. The father continued to resist and it was clear to me that the officer was going to arrest the man concerned.

Had he been arrested that morning, the consequences for this man, the other parents and the school would have been very serious. As the police officer held on to the man, I succeeded in pulling the man free and escorting him into the school with his little girl still hanging on to his hand.

When the parents had returned down the road, I went to the officer involved in the incident near the school gate. His point was that the man had walked on the footpath instead of the road! Most people would hold that footpaths are for walking on while roads carry traffic. I was invited to lodge a complaint about the incident.

Soon after this upsetting incident, word spread that one of the parents had gone on hunger strike in connection with the school protest. I quickly discovered that it was the same man who had been pushed off the footpath. His wife greeted me silently at the house when I called. She was utterly traumatised by the decision taken by her husband. The children in the family were sent to stay with relatives and kept away as much as possible from this worrying scene.

The man on hunger strike was calm and composed. He told me of his desperation and how all efforts to protect the children, including his daughter, had not succeeded in ending the brutality being daily suffered by them. In his own estimation he was a failure as a parent. He chose the option of hunger strike as his way of highlighting the ongoing unacceptable situation.

He felt that, by ending his life, he would be saying sorry to his little girl for not being able to protect her and would also highlight the awful events that had begun in June 2001. It was heartbreaking to listen to this good man who was broken in spirit and saw no other course of action open to him. He could appreciate that his children and his wife would be deprived of a father and husband should he go through to the end with his hunger strike, but he still saw his action as being justified in the light of the circumstances of his family when the protest at his daughter's school had begun.

This was new territory for me. All I could do was spend as much time as possible with him, his wife and other relatives. He was always unfailingly courteous and welcoming whenever I came to visit. He was pleased to be blessed and prayed with during each visit. I could see the pain in his eyes and the fear in the eyes of his wife. She could not have been more supportive and helpful.

The days began to pass and I could see that he was reaching a point where it might be difficult to get him to end his hunger strike. To assist me, I sought some valuable information and understanding from a former hunger striker who was able to give me a unique insight into the dynamics of hunger strike.

After a few days, the man agreed to go to his local doctor for medical examination. All efforts made to change his mind and end his hunger strike failed. By this stage, it was extremely worrying. Others who knew the identity of the man worked hard to help but to no avail.

One evening, in a conversation with him and his wife, I again raised the issue of what his death was going to achieve. His hope was that it would highlight the plight of the children and the failure to stop the hurt being daily inflicted on them. I asked him if he would be prepared to end his protest if his message were put into the public domain. He wasn't sure.

That night I made contact with a TV reporter. I asked her if it would be possible to carry out an interview with the hunger striker so that he could say his piece and thereby save his life. She was not sure and would have to get a ruling from the television company. This was the only time I asked any favour from any media organisation. I was extremely grateful to the reporter and the organisation for co-operating in this difficult situation.

The decision of the broadcaster was to carry an interview with the man, and I would be interviewed immediately afterwards about the situation as I saw it. This arrangement was accepted by all concerned, but the hunger striker wanted the interview to be held in Holy Cross Monastery. He was fearful that his house could be located if he did the interview at home. He came for the interview on condition that the broadcaster did not show his face or any identifying characteristics. The interviewer conducted a most sensitive and professional interview. She could not have done more in an extremely difficult situation.

The interviews were broadcast that same night on the late news, but we were not out of the woods yet. There were a few difficult hours when he changed his mind about ending the hunger strike because of press reports. It was clear that he was getting weaker by the hour and his capacity to decide to end the hunger strike was becoming more doubtful. It was to our enormous relief that he finally said that he was ending it and that he would get medical advice on how best to return to eating. His wife had her husband back and the children had their father back. It took some days for him to recover his strength. The courage and support of this man's wife was truly admirable. Circumstances sometimes bring out qualities in a person that might otherwise not be recognised in the ordinary ebb and flow of daily life.

This incident alerted other parents to the fact that their situation had gone on too long. If we had now reached the stage where a parent was prepared to take his own life, we were into a new and very dangerous phase of the protest.

My own disappointment was that now we were into our third month since the return after the summer holidays. However, there were some blessings for which we were thankful. Apart from the sad event of the police officer being hurt by the blast bomb, nobody else had been physically injured or killed. The school was operating at an exceptionally high level and the teachers and staff were present every day.

Some parents still remained each day in the school, so great was their concern for the safety of their children during the school day. Other parents spent some hours together at Holy Cross Monastery where various stress-reduction activities were gradually introduced. Others were working and so had to keep in contact with the situation by means of media reports and phone calls.

We welcomed one great light that shone into an otherwise bleak situation. It was the visit to Holy Cross School of Archbishop Desmond Tutu, retired Anglican Archbishop of Johannesburg. He was in Belfast for a visit and had spoken the previous day at the Wellington Park Hotel at an event to which Fr Gary and I were invited.

It was a marvel to watch him pray with the children, dance, talk, and laugh and relate to them in a most wonderfully warm way. His presence among us was a great blessing and was a great honour for me to meet someone whom I had admired so much since my first visit to South Africa in 1978.

Some of the pupils summed up his visit very well as only children can:

'He was really fun; he told us jokes and was dancing around and running about.' [Orlaith: *Irish News*, 8 November 2001]

He said long ago he had people who said things against him and God told him to pray for them. He said that if someone kicks you not to kick them back, just pray for them.

He raised his hands in the air when he prayed and he told us that was the only time you should ever raise you hand – to pray.' [Nicole: *Irish News*, 8 November 2001]

Desmond Tutu also met with the residents of Glenbryn at Stormont and listened to their concerns and issues. A spokesperson for them summed up their meeting by saying that they found him a very warm man who listened to them.

Archbishop Tutu described the protest as being 'very, very close to a solution'. One of his counsels will always remain with me and that was to maintain a link, no matter how fragile, between poles that are apart. His own experience during the many years of apartheid in South

Africa had taught him great patience and never to lose hope. We said goodbye to him, the better for having met him.

Unfortunately, it would still be some time before we would reach a suspension of the protest. An issue that now faced the school was how best to deal with the pupils who were to sit their 11+ examination, due to take place on 9 November. This examination would determine the school a child would attend for second-level education. It is a great blessing that this examination will soon be phased out to make way for a better form of assessment.

The protestors had talked about suspending the protest on that day to allow the children to go to school in peace and quiet. This was appreciated but, after months of protest and very little progress made, there was still great mistrust. However, another factor came into play that put the suspension in some doubt.

An unidentified parent and her seven-year-old daughter initiated legal proceedings on 7 November 2001, against the Secretary of State, Dr John Reid, and the police, among others, for failing to identify and arrest protestors for breaking the law. She could no longer cope with the situation and acknowledged that everything to stop the children from being targeted had been to no avail. In her sworn affidavit she pointed out that the erection of screens could have prevented the protestors from getting within touching distance of the children.

It had been my hope to take this legal action to save a parent from having to put herself in a difficult position. However, I was told that because I belong to a religious order, it was unlikely that I would qualify for legal aid. The mother who took this action is a brave lady and, in fact, had to leave Ardoyne shortly afterwards because of threats she received.

The Concerned Residents of Upper Ardoyne issued a statement saying that this legal challenge put the suspension for the 11+ examination in jeopardy. On the day of the examination, Mrs Tanney had the children brought to school by car so as to avoid any upset to them. The protestors reacted negatively to this and complained that there was not much point in suspending the protest if the children went to school in this way. In the event, those who sat the examination in 2001 did extremely well despite the difficulties of studying and preparing for it during such a traumatic time.

Another week ended with no end in sight but efforts were constantly being made to find a way out for the children. On 13 November, the police set up a review of security in the Ardoyne area. District Commander Maxwell was asked by the Chief Constable to complete this review by 23 November. Views would be accepted in writing or by phone or at a face-to-face meeting.

There was still a long way to go before the children would be rescued from their daily suffering as they went to and from their school.

CHAPTER EIGHT

I BELIEVE IN the work of the Holy Spirit. Since 3 September 2001, when I was asked to walk with the children and parents I had never believed that we were doing anything other than what children and parents do all over the world – seeking an education for the young. Various commentators saw this as 'Drumcree part 2'. Others saw it as a paramilitary or political infiltration of what seemed an innocent walk to and from school. People are free to believe as they wish.

Indeed, Rt Rev Alan Harper, a Church of Ireland bishop, is reported as acknowledging the serious and unacceptable abuse suffered by the children while also speaking of there being political exploitation on both sides of the divide. He expressed the view that the trauma suffered by the Holy Cross children was made much worse by the politicisation and orchestrated media hype that attended the situation. It is true that local politicians were present daily on Ardoyne Road but the nationalist MLAs, Alban Maginnis (SDLP) and Gerry Kelly (Sinn Féin) chose not to walk.

Truthfully, before God, I can only state that nothing else was going on behind the scenes. There was no master plan to achieve some other objective behind or beyond what seemed to be happening. Sometimes the truth seems too simple to believe. To my last breath, I will go on believing that the right of the children to an education as chosen by their parents was all that was happening. Of course, it is possible that people would have liked to infiltrate such a respectable activity and divert it to other purposes.

One man who had lived through the worst days of the Troubles expressed the opinion that the presence of clergy on a daily basis with the people had saved the situation, preventing it from deteriorating into bloodshed. It was an enormous compliment and, if true, worth every minute spent on Ardoyne Road over those months.

By the end of October, everyone, as we have seen was tired and needed a break. This applied to protestor as well as to parent and child.

One morning in early November, I woke up at 2.30 a.m. I will always remember the time as I suddenly became aware that the protest could end more quickly than anyone had predicted. We, Holy Cross School, and not the protestors would end the protest!

What dawned on me was that over the previous two months we had been sucked into a living drama. We all had roles to play. The children dressed up in their school uniforms of red, grey and white every morning. The parents got ready and walked to the assembly point where they met soldiers and police, also in uniform. Then the two priests arrived, also in uniform. The media had microphones, cameras and pencils at the ready in case the normal did not happen. In other words, there were 'actors', 'scenes' and 'acts' that followed an increasingly predictable script.

Before we moved off, the protestors got into position. The police officer in charge was cast in the role of Master of Ceremonies, who checked that all was ready before giving us our cue to move off slowly. The police too had their rehearsed part to play.

The protestors knew their lines off by heart. We knew our place on the road by now. The police knew where to walk and how to react once we all kept to the script and to the prearranged moves. Only if anyone moved out of place, as on the morning that the father and child went on the footpath, would there be need to think and take action. It had become so predictable.

What if we were to refuse to play our parts any longer? Suppose we declared that the drama was over and that we were withdrawing our co-operation from what had become a worldwide offensive charade. In so far as I had any role to play my shame was increasing by the day. It was not that I was in charge, but because of my role, both as chair of school governors and parish priest, it was weighing heavier and heavier on my conscience that this abomination was continuing.

The thoughts as I lay there in bed came flooding one after another. Suppose we refused to form up in line at 8.45 every morning and wait. We would refuse to accept that we were not free to move toward the school until allowed. If we were breaking the law or parading illegally, we could have no argument with restrictions such as these. But we were a totally peaceful group who wanted to go to school and home again. Was that too much to ask?

The advantage to this inspiration of the Holy Spirit was that we could help the residents of Glenbryn to stop digging in deeper. They needed a helping hand out of their predicament. Understandably, an offer of help from us could not be made or received. But suppose we were to announce our decision to withdraw from the daily charade that had developed. As I lay there, I could not but wonder whether if this course of action had been taken on 20 June and on the days until school closed at the end of June, the September situation might not actually have been necessary. It is impossible for me to answer this as I was still in Italy at the time. Only those who were there at the time can tell us their reasons for doing as they did.

By now the hopes of sleep had gone. Out of bed I got and went on my knees to ask that same Holy Spirit for guidance. It became clear to me that the parents would be the arbiters of this course of action. After all, it was their children who were having the basic right of an education threatened and who were being put in danger every day. If they agreed, the school governors, the teachers and staff of the school would need to be brought on board. I was not at all certain what the outcome would be, but, it was worth testing the idea and seeing what emerged.

A meeting with the parents was taking place in the Ardoyne Community Centre a few evenings later. This was one of the regular meetings held so that groups like the Right to Education Group, the governors, local political representatives, parents or whoever wished to speak could contribute to both assessment and suggestions of a way forward.

This regular coming together was one of the great strengths of those months. Here we had a community in crisis but united in a common determination to stand firm for the education of their children. The next time I saw the people of Ardoyne come together was in Spring 2004, following a number of tragic suicides in the area. From the depth of grief there arose again solidarity in the face of the silent killer that is suicide.

When it came to my turn to speak, I moved to the microphone with a considerable degree of apprehension. I knew what I was going to propose but I had no way of knowing what the response would be. It was always a danger that a bad situation might be made worse. In as simple a way as I could, I put forward the possibility of us ending the protest instead of asking others to declare it over. I could see the look of bewilderment on most faces as I outlined what had come to me a few nights earlier. In finishing, I asked if we could discuss this as a proposal which, if agreed upon, I would tell the police about the next day.

As I finished there were no questions. The parents rose to their feet and gave a standing ovation to express their approval. It was a most amazing moment as they voted with their hands and feet. It was at that moment that I knew we had been visited by the Holy Spirit who would rescue the children out of the horror they were in and that was set to continue for months if rumours circulating were true. It had been said that the protest would go on until June 2002 at least.

Now the pressure was really on. The parents could see some hope of an end and rightly did not want any delay. Discussions with the governors and school were all positive. It cannot be said often enough that the rock-like support of the school governors gave me encouragement and strength as it had since I had first joined their ranks on 6 August.

The next step would be to approach the police and seek their assessment. After all the school governors were bound to ensure the health and safety of the children. If we were to put them into foreseeable danger, we would be acting irresponsibly and would have a lot to answer for should things go wrong.

A meeting was arranged with Assistant Chief Constable Alan McQuillan and Commander Roger Maxwell. They listened with their customary courtesy but found it hard to believe that I was serious about what was being proposed. In fact, they did not hold out much hope of success. Alan McQuillan was due to travel on business next day and so no immediate decision could be taken.

Days went past and still no news came from the police, so another meeting with them was arranged. This time it was not a question of asking about our proposal but of saying that the decision had been taken and that we would go ahead with our plan for non-co-operation. Of course, we would need to prepare very carefully for this approach as the paramount concern was the safety of the children.

The police asked for a few days to see if they could test this out with the Glenbryn residents. It seemed strange to me that just as the previous discussions at mid-term break had taken place with the protesting community, the same was to happen again – it would have made more sense to listen and accept the decisions of the parents who had broken no law.

Eventually the police reported back that the plan as we had proposed it would not be acceptable. But if there was some political action as well, there was a possibility that some progress could be made towards bringing the protest to an end. We had not given up on the plan to end our participation in the daily drama but we prepared to consider other options that might help.

The governors decided to initiate a series of meetings with all the political parties in the Northern Ireland Assembly. As chair of governors, I wrote to the leader of each party asking that we meet, with a view to exerting political pressure to bring the protest against the children and the school to an end. Letters were sent to the Rev. Ian Paisley (DUP), Gerry Adams, (Sinn Féin), Monica McWilliams (Northern Ireland Women's Coalition), David Trimble (Ulster Unionist Party), Mark Durkan (SDLP), David Ervine (Progressive Unionist Party) and David Ford (Alliance Party).

Some of these responded almost at once and arrangements were made to meet. Some of the meetings were held in Holy Cross School and others in Holy Cross Monastery. By the time the protest was suspended a few of the party leaders had not been able to meet the school governors and, in fact, met them after that date. There was a small number that we did not meet due to various circumstances.

Traditionally the Catholic Church is rightly careful to avoid party political favour or giving the impression of being too close to any one party. It was clear to all who were being hurt by this protest that urgent action had been needed since 19 June. Now it was November and still the children and their parents trudged to and from school each day in truly appalling circumstances. As already mentioned, some politicians had been most supportive and concerned.

Indeed, on one occasion, a potentially serious situation was diffused by the actions of a political party leader. It was made known that, as a sign of support, some secondary schools in West Belfast were being asked on a specified day to come to Ardoyne to show solidarity with the children of Holy Cross. It was a magnificent gesture and deeply appreciated by the parents and the school. However, the difficulty was that there was the potential for violence or some disorder by having so many people – the majority young people – on the streets of North Belfast. In other circumstances, such a demonstration of caring would have been welcomed with open arms. But, the core issue was the safety of both the young pupils who would come from West Belfast and the children of Holy Cross.

I made contact with Martin McGuinness, then Minister for Education at Stormont, and asked for a meeting with him to discuss what was to happen the following morning. He responded immediately and came to Holy Cross Monastery to discuss the matter. He shared the concern about the potential for violence and assured me that he would see what could be done. He wanted to acknowledge the sentiment of solidarity and its expression while at the same time ensuring that nobody was put in danger by having such a great crowd of people on the street.

The next morning, I was informed that a representative adult group from West Belfast would arrive in Ardoyne to express concern at what was happening to the Holy Cross children and their parents. Gerry Adams, president of Sinn Féin, would also be present. It was suggested that I should make a short address of thanks to the people who had arrived to show support.

As I arrived at the Ardoyne shops to address the people who had arrived, I realised that it would be difficult to speak to so many in the open air. I was no Daniel O'Connell for large outdoor meetings. A helpful press photographer offered me a small ladder to use, in order that I could speak my words to the assembled people.

It was encouraging to find so many people who had bothered to come across to Ardoyne and just say how much they cared and how hurt they were to see children caught up in this awful event. Most were parents themselves and could appreciate what the men and women of Ardoyne were going through as they saw their children come under such pressure.

It was a great honour to thank these people and to assure them that their care and concern would be remembered by the people of Ardoyne. I finished the few words by giving a blessing. Then those present dispersed with dignity and in a quiet fashion. A potentially difficult situation had passed off as a moment of true solidarity and prayer.

In the broader political arena, it became important to deal with the office of the First and Deputy First Ministers. Without their input it would be difficult to put together a package that could be presented to the people of Glenbryn. As I have stated several times, it was a fundamental point of the school governors never to negotiate while the children were still in danger. It was morally reprehensible to bargain on the backs of children. That is why I was constantly worried when I heard talk of reciprocation as if the children had something to offer or had offended in some way.

Meeting with David Trimble and Mark Durkan, along with their officials in Stormont, led to the possibility of a package of measures being put together for the people of Glenbryn and also for Holy Cross School. We would have wished to take a different approach and have an end to the protest before dealing with this. However, by this stage we were not going to oppose the preparation of a package of measures aimed principally at addressing the issues of the Glenbryn residents.

As these discussions were reported back to the parents at our regular meetings, the opinion was expressed that the bad behaviour of the protestors was being rewarded. This was a legitimate interpretation of what was being proposed, but the alternative was for the school governors to refuse to co-operate with any such moves and be accused of refusing to work towards a resolution of the protest.

As moves towards a resolution of the protest seemed to be gaining momentum, another meeting with representatives of the Glenbryn residents took place on Wednesday, 14 November. The venue was the Everton Complex, Crumlin Road. As long as we were talking to each other there was always hope. No matter how painfully slow progress might have seemed, there was never any alternative to dialogue. The Glenbryn representatives were also searching for a way forward and our meeting with them was one of a series of nine meetings planned by them to take place during that week. Included in these would be a meeting with the Secretary of State and one with the First and Deputy First Ministers.

I was able to report that, since our last meeting a group of parents along with the school governors had met with the PSNI. In this meeting, a series of steps had been agreed that it was hoped would help bring some normality back into the area and improve the current situation. The parents had been asked to consider three forms of transporting the children to and from school – Belfast Education and Library Board (BELB) buses, taxis and walking. If buses or taxis were used, it would be necessary for those parents who chose to walk to do so on the footpath. The plan was that if these options worked well, the use of private cars would be considered. To avoid cars parking on the Ardoyne Road in the mornings or afternoons, while pupils were left off at the school or collected, it had been agreed that a turning point would be created in the school grounds. It was hoped that this would alleviate some of the concerns of the Glenbryn residents.

The agreement by parents not to stop their cars at all on Ardoyne Road near the school was a gesture of goodwill. However, the school governors were greatly concerned about allowing cars into the school grounds on health and safety grounds. Also, the creation of a turning circle for cars would mean sacrificing the playground in front of the school. But as we looked at the totality of the situation and the severity of the effects the protest was having on the children we felt it necessary to support the proposals.

One of the difficulties that had to be faced was that Holy Cross School entrance would now have a single access for both pedestrians and cars. BELB officials had visited the school and had confirmed that by moving the school gates and carrying out some other renovations to the grounds it would be possible to create a turning point for cars and a safe area for pedestrians.

The Glenbryn group wanted the arrangement for the cars entering the school grounds to be put into effect immediately. In the interests of the safety of the local residents, they asked that the parking of cars on Ardoyne Road on either side of the school be discouraged. They also raised the possibility of a through road leading from St Gabriel's College into the grounds of Holy Cross School, but it was pointed out that the use of St Gabriel's grounds had been agreed as a short-term measure and, while the college had temporarily sacrificed the use of its pitch, it needed to return to operating normally.

We learned from the Glenbryn group about plans to have speed ramps completed on Ardoyne Road by Friday, 16 November. It was significant that the protestors wished that parents be alerted about this arrangement to prevent any surprise – they were seeking to reach out in some way.

The meeting ended with both parties agreeing that everyone involved should be focused on achieving a return to normality. While there was a basis for progress towards a resolution, it was acknowledged that, in order to achieve this, there were significant difficulties which needed to be overcome. The Glenbryn representatives concluded by stating that their intentions in attempting to resolve the protest were sincere, and that efforts would continue in the coming days. It might seem that a lot is being made out of very little, but in this situation, this far into the protest, it was significant that tiny steps were being taken towards rebuilding trust.

To bring as much attention as possible to the plight of the children, the Right to Education Group called a public rally in the centre of Belfast at the City Hall, to take place on Friday, 23 November at 4 p.m. It was a great privilege for me to be asked to address the rally along with other speakers. Eamon McCann came from Derry to lend his voice to the cause of the children. Speaking from the back of a lorry on a Friday afternoon in the middle of Belfast was a daunting task. The courage of the mother of a pupil who spoke and her clear and direct message of calling for an end to the protest were inspiring. My own few words were along the same lines and came from the heart.

Meanwhile, at meetings with the office of First and Deputy First Ministers at Stormont, the school governors were kept abreast of developments. While we could not enter into any form of negotiations while the children were still being subjected to a daily protest, we had a responsibility to facilitate the drawing up of proposals which, if accepted by the Glenbryn residents, would also be acceptable to the parents and to the school. This was delicate in the extreme as there was still very little trust across the divide. As has been shown, our effort to engage in real dialogue was at an initial stage.

As November drew to a close there was the prospect that if the protest did not end before Christmas, there could be even greater difficulty finding a solution in the New Year. Over the three months that I had been with the parents and children, I had come to admire so much their dignity and restraint. Could this last indefinitely?

After the midterm break I had noticed a difference. There was an impatience creeping in among some of the parents. The daily walk in a crowd, having to wait until allowed to proceed and the daily taunting were wearing on all our nerves. Little by little, I perceived that the time could be near when parents might refuse to wait for a resolution.

One afternoon, as we lined up to return with the children, a father took his child and began to walk down the road before the whole group was ready. Fearing for his safety, I asked him if he would wait. He told me that he had waited since June 2001 to be allowed to walk to and from school with his daughter and he was waiting no longer. He reminded me of my own suggestion that we no longer play our 'roles' in this daily drama. A police officer had to restrain him physically from proceeding on down the road. The incident ended peacefully but it confirmed my impression that whatever leadership and support I was giving might not be enough for much longer. This worried me because if a few parents decided that they were waiting no longer, we were into new territory.

For this reason, the proposals to be put to the protestors could not come soon enough. At the same time, as we had nothing to bargain with, we had to be sure that the good of the school and the wider community of Ardoyne was not damaged in any way by the politicians' proposals.

On 23 November, the Office of the First and Deputy First Minister wrote to the Glenbryn residents, the parents and school governors. The letter was from David Trimble and Mark Durkan, who held those posts at that time. They began by saying that their letter flowed 'from the very helpful and constructive discussions we have held this week with Nigel Dodds, the North Belfast MLAs, the Holy Cross Board of Governors, the Right to Education Group and the Glenbryn Residents.'

They made it clear that they wanted the protest at Holy Cross School to end and on a basis which would ensure no resumption. They also stated their commitment to tackling the socio-economic problems facing North Belfast. All recipients were asked not to comment publicly on the contents of the letter as the Glenbryn residents were holding a public meeting that evening to consider whether to end the protest or not. For the parents, this would be a crucial time and one of great anxiety. If an end were in sight, there would be enormous relief. If not, the prospects looked extremely bleak.

The issues raised in the letter fell into five main categories.

1. Under the heading of 'Community Safety' there was recognition that traffic-calming measures on Ardoyne Road and other changes at the Alliance Avenue-Ardoyne Road intersection would improve the overall appearance of the area and enhance community safety. Proposed time targets were set out and the hope was to have these works completed soon.

2. 'Community Infrastructure' highlighted the fact that throughout North Belfast there existed a need to improve the capacity of local communities to plan the future, interact with local agencies and ensure that all applications for grants and funding be well presented.

   A North Belfast Community Action Project was announced. The aim was to plan short, medium and long-term actions to address social and community issues in North Belfast; the project was to identify ways of offering further support to community activities already working well. It was to have an immediate outreach advisory service to ensure that all areas would take full advantage of existing or upcoming European programmes.

When the members of this Action Project were appointed they were: Rev John Dunlop, then at Rosemount Presbyterian Church in North Belfast; Monsignor Tom Toner, Administrator of St Peter's Cathedral in West Belfast; and Roy Adams, a civil servant. The project was a joint initiative of the Office of First and Deputy First Ministers and the Department of Social Development.

After a wide and intensive consultation, the Action Project's report was published in May 2002. Nobody who saw this group tackle its task could doubt the determination of these men to do the best possible for North Belfast. My regret was that the Catholic representation did not come from within North Belfast. Never did I want or expect to be appointed to this group myself, but there are so many hardworking Catholic clergy and lay people around who could have contributed to improving life in North Belfast.

3. Under 'Education and Counselling', schools in North Belfast would provide the focus. It was recognised that Holy Cross Girls' and Wheatfield Schools were deeply affected by the disturbances across North Belfast which had impacted on children and staff.

It was also recognised that relationships built up between schools had been badly affected. To address these issues it was proposed to provide additional support to pupils and staff in affected schools in North Belfast, to assist them in dealing with the stress and trauma their pupils and staff had suffered. Additional resources would also be provided to schools and the youth services to assist the re-establishment and further development of relationships between communities in the area. Counselling services were also promised to the schools.

4. Local issues were listed in an appendix to the letter of 23 November 2001. These included the protection for house windows at interfaces. The playing fields at Ballysillan would have missing bollards replaced on the boundary adjacent to

Wheatfield School. A transport community scheme was promised that would enable scheduled services to shops, amenities and public services for Glenbryn residents. A dedicated co-ordinator was to be appointed to develop community infrastructure in selected areas. There were a few other local issues, too, affecting principally the improvement of life for residents of the area.

5. The fifth issue to be addressed was policing. Policing and security matters were outside the remit of the Northern Ireland Executive, belonging as they do to the Secretary of State and the PSNI. The PSNI had already informed the Executive that it would provide a dedicated 24-hour community policing unit and develop a police community relations programme if the protest ended.

Work to heighten and extend the 'peace wall' between Glenbryn and Alliance Avenue had already begun and was scheduled to finish after Christmas. As mentioned previously, some years earlier there had been a request by the Glenbryn residents for a separating wall with a locked gate across Ardoyne Road. There was no mention of this in the letter, and the attached appendix did not contain any reference to the re-introduction of this proposal. As will be seen later, this matter became a contentious issue in 2002 and raised fears that the protest might be re-ignited.

Much of the violence in the area took place at weekends. In response, the PSNI promised a static policing point at the interface of Ardoyne Road and Alliance Avenue. This would come into existence only if the protest ended.

The letter from David Trimble and Mark Durkan encouraged all to help put in place appropriate structures such as a joint community forum for necessary community dialogue. These proposals were to be discussed by the Executive on Monday, 26 November. Of course, the nature of these discussions would be affected by the acceptance or rejection of the proposals at the Friday night meeting of the Glenbryn residents. All we could do at this stage was wait and pray.

Some in Ardoyne saw in the proposals a reinforcement of their opinion that the bad behaviour of the protestors was being rewarded. My own view remained that the acceptance of these proposals by those protesting would provide an opportunity to get the children out of their nightmare for the first time since 19 June. It was not a case of accepting anything that would be unjust or unfair. But in truth none of the promises in the letter of 23 November were in proportion to what had happened.

Friday evening came and the people of Glenbryn gathered to discuss the proposals outlined above. The meeting was limited to residents and so it was not easy to gain any information about what reception the proposals were receiving. It is difficult to believe how close the two sides of the community in Ardoyne live to each other.

The wait seemed interminable. There was an event in the GAA clubhouse in Flax Street to which I had been invited, but until the verdict of the meeting was known I found it impossible to go anywhere. It was not easy to watch TV or read or settle down to anything. If the Glenbryn meeting accepted the proposals, what a relief it would be for the children, parents and the whole community of Ardoyne. If the vote went against the proposals, then where would we go? We already knew that we had no intention of continuing the 'drama' any longer.

Shortly after 11 p.m., a journalist phoned me to say that the meeting in Glenbryn had just finished. I remember closing my eyes as I waited for the next sentence: 'The proposals have been accepted and the protest is being suspended.'

Months of protest were being put on hold. My immediate reaction was a silent prayer of thanksgiving to God for such truly good news. The Holy Spirit had delivered once again, if not in the way I had imagined.

The phone started ringing as journalists sought a reaction on behalf of the governors. We welcomed the news with enormous relief and delight. But it was also necessary to point out that we had a huge test ahead of us as we sought to rebuild an almost total breakdown of trust. We would have to learn how to manage a more normal situation such as had not existed since the previous June. Even in those first moments of utter relief it was necessary to point out that a lot of sensitive cross-community work would have to begin. This, I suggested, could prove more difficult than as set out on paper. It would take generosity on both sides.

Someone asked me did I not worry that the word used was to 'suspend' the protest rather than to 'end' the protest. While some commentators cast doubt on whether the protest was really over, I believed from the start that the intention was to have an end to the protest. It seemed to me that we were all being asked to move slowly and to take small steps. To 'suspend' the protest may have been easier for the residents of Glenbryn to accept than to 'end' it.

The local MP, Nigel Dodds, welcomed the residents' announcement, adding, 'This is a lesson to the Government that if problems are allowed to simmer away and fester, rather than be dealt with, you leave yourself open to something like this happening.' [*Belfast Telegraph*, 24 November 2001, p.1]

Gerry Kelly, of Sinn Féin, expressed his hope that if a communications structure were put in place in Ardoyne, that it could be replicated in other parts of Belfast. Other politicians and community leaders from all sides expressed relief that the protest would not be continuing.

Most people saw in the suspension of the protest an indication of the power of dialogue. Since the beginning of September, the children and parents had been under a dark cloud that covered not just Ardoyne Road but people much further away. People living nowhere near North Belfast had become involved in what was happening.

As we have seen, some people were firmly on the side of the children, while others took another viewpoint. But on that Friday night all must have been united in utter relief that we would not face each other across Ardoyne Road from Monday onwards.

Many of the children were already asleep when the news broke and so would learn only the next morning that their daily suffering was over.

After midnight, I joined Fr Gary in the GAA club. Rumours were rife that the protest was over and I was invited to speak to those present. It was with tears in my eyes that I gave the news that the protest had been suspended. The relief and joy of all present were tangible and people stood to applaud the news.

Early that Saturday morning, as I went to bed, I knew much remained to be done in preparation for the children going to school on Monday morning. Now they would be able to get back to the way children go to school all over the world. It was to be hoped that a new dawn awaited us.

CHAPTER NINE

THE SATURDAY MORNING after the suspension of the protest was strange. It took a few minutes to realise that it was over and that, all going well, there would be no harassment of the children on Monday.

There were many enquiries from the media during the day regarding plans for Monday morning. Many interviewers harped on the use of the word 'suspended' as opposed to 'ended'. Some of the local people at the shops in Ardoyne made the same observation and wondered could we trust that the children were safe to go to school without hindrance.

My own opinion from the moment I heard the statement was that the protest was over, at least in the form we had known it. I could see that those in Glenbryn who wanted to 'sell' the deal at the meeting had to bring on board some in their community who wanted to go on with the protest. To 'suspend' the protest was more palatable to some than to say it was over. I could understand this and while the parents and all of us would have been more secure with a more final statement, there was enough to go on with.

It was strange to look up Ardoyne Road on that Saturday morning. While the police and army jeeps were still around, the paths were empty and the road looked so normal. It was hard to believe that, just twenty-four hours earlier, this had still been the scene of real danger to children going to school. I could only utter a prayer of thanksgiving to God and to people of good will who had done so much to bring about this wonderful new dawn.

That Saturday afternoon, I drove to Dublin to attend a meeting and to visit my family, whom I had scarcely seen since my father's death. As I arrived in Dublin, I got a phone call from the Glenbryn protestor to whom I had given my number. He chatted for a few moments about the reaction among his neighbours and asked how things were in Holy Cross. Then he suggested that we should have a meeting on the Sunday to arrange a code of conduct for Ardoyne Road that would help avoid any recurrence of the protest. His concern was that after a protest stretching back to June, it would not be easy to return to normality overnight. He was absolutely right and I was delighted to assure him of our co-operation. I didn't tell him that I was in Dublin, and I thanked God for mobile phones!

Again, it was necessary to find a neutral venue for this meeting. It would be impossible to hold it in Holy Cross Hall as the residents of Glenbryn would find this unacceptable, and the community centre in Glenbryn would have been unacceptable to the parents. In the end, we agreed that the Council Chamber in City Hall would be acceptable to all concerned. We agreed to have about ten people on each delegation for these crucial talks. For many who would participate, this was the first face-to-face meeting since the protest began. It would be painful in a particular way for parents who had suffered seeing what had happened to their children. The protestors also had their fears and hurts.

Because I was in Dublin for the next few hours, I asked Fr Gary to organise governor and parent members for the meeting the following day in City Hall. By the time I got home later that night, all was ready for the encounter.

There was only one topic of conversation as I greeted people as they came to Mass that Sunday morning. There was a tangible relief that the children were out of the daily harassment. Others expressed anger that remained because of what had happened. Still others were worried that the protest would restart at the first possible opportunity. These varying attitudes were to be expected and helped me to realise that much remained to be done. We were not out of the woods yet.

Belfast on a Sunday afternoon is not the liveliest of places. Sunday,

25 November, was no exception as we made our way into the City Hall. The Council Chamber is an impressive place with all the trappings of British administration. We were glad to be welcomed to this place and to realise that the city of Belfast would be deeply affected by how we succeeded or not that afternoon.

My fear was that if the talks should break down, there was always the danger that the protest could recommence. It was a thought no side wished to contemplate.

The meeting began in a hesitant way and took some time to make progress. Our main concern was that we would find a way of resolving any issues that arose on Ardoyne Road in the coming days and weeks leading up to the Christmas holidays. We listened to the concerns expressed on both sides and agreed that a breakdown was in nobody's interest.

It is important to remember that even though we were all in the same place, with an agreed agenda, there was very little trust. It was to be expected that caution would be exercised and suspicion was never far away. It is to the credit of both sides, that after a few hours, we reached agreement that gave us enough confidence to believe that a peaceful return to school was possible.

The agreement reached was simple but sensible. Nobody would say or do anything that would jeopardise the fragile peace. Should anyone have a complaint, it was not to be fought out on the road but recorded so that it could be resolved through dialogue and not through violence that would achieve nothing. Holy Cross School found that the keeping of an 'Incident Book' was an important factor in dealing with complaints of unacceptable behaviour.

Of course, there was no guarantee that even with our meeting going well, the same would happen the following morning. Nervousness and worry would be inevitable. I met with the police to discuss details of what would happen from a security perspective on Monday morning.

It should be remembered that the suspension of the protest was a huge relief for the police. Some of them had been associated with policing the protest from its beginning. To this day, I still meet police officers who tell me that they walked Ardoyne Road during the protest

— because they wore balaclavas, there was only a handful of officers whose faces I actually saw during the walks. In addition, to the personal relief of police officers, there would be a great saving within the security budget should the protest end.

Over that weekend also, the other schools in the parish and the area must have been relieved that the disruption of the past months seemed to be over. Many people had to make detours to get to other schools and to work because of the protest. I can recall buses being delayed because of the necessity for the parents to assemble on the road before being allowed to proceed to the school. It was hoped all that would be a thing of the past.

As always, the parents would be the ones to decide what to do on the Monday morning. Some were concerned and decided that they would not take their child to school that first day for fear that there would be trouble. This was most understandable in the light of what they had been through. The vast majority decided to make an act of trust and go to school.

On Monday, 26 November, a new era began as families prepared for school. There was a media presence there to report what would happen. There is a curved wall on the Ardoyne side of Alliance Avenue, and during the protest it was christened 'the wailing wall'. Around this wall, parents, children, relatives and neighbours would gather to prepare for the walk to school. Indeed, some mornings and afternoons, there were tears. I vividly remember a mother and her little girl taking cover one afternoon beside the mudguard of an army vehicle, to avoid stones being thrown from Glenbryn. When the stones were no longer a danger, the little girl was too afraid to come out from beside the army personnel carrier. It took persuasion to get her to believe that she would be safe.

On this particular Monday, almost by habit, the parents, pupils and relatives gathered in the shadow of the 'wailing wall' to ponder what they would do on the first morning since 20 June on which they were promised that there would not be a protest. The atmosphere was different, with a mixture of utter relief that the situation looked more normal combined with a fear that appearances could be deceptive. It is not easy to feel confident after enduring months of angry protest just to get to school.

Any of us who had been at the meeting in City Hall the previous evening did our best to give a summary of what had been said and what had been promised. It was not possible to reach all parents, though. It was humbling for me when a father or a mother would ask, 'Father, what do you think? Is it safe?' All I could say was that I believed it was.

While some parents walked ahead on their own, many moved off in groups. There were pushchairs to be manoeuvred and children's hands to be held tightly. That first morning, very few parents availed of the school bus provided by the BELB. Members of the media were more interested in the bus than the parents.

Of course, as it was the first day without a protest, there were scores of police along Ardoyne Road; these were backed up by army patrols. But there were no armoured vehicle barriers and no riot squad escorts for the walk to school. Still, the arrival at the gate of the school could not come soon enough. It was, as always, open in welcome and there was Anne Tanney together with her teaching and school staff waiting to receive their beloved pupils. Thanks to so many people on all sides, the first walk to school without protest worked.

My own delight and relief as I saw the parents return back down the road in twos and threes was tinged with sadness. To reduce any tension that might have been caused had Fr Gary or I walked up the road, we had decided to wait at the 'wailing wall' to ensure that the parents came back safely. And they did. They were so relieved. Not since that day has either Fr Gary or I walked from our parish to Holy Cross Girls' School along Ardoyne Road. Nobody ever said we couldn't or shouldn't, but it was the parents who had asked us to walk with them in the first instance, and now to eliminate any possible extra danger to parents or children, not walking with them is a small price to pay.

In fairness, it must be recorded that the suspension of the loyalist protest had been delivered. It would have been so easy for this fragile negotiated settlement to be sabotaged. To this day, this area of North Belfast remains volatile but, at long last, Ardoyne Road had reverted to being the normal school route it had been for the previous thirty-two years. As I stood there watching this transformation, my faith in humanity was bolstered so much. Here, walking past each other in relative peace, were people who the previous week had been locked into a conflict that seemed beyond immediate resolution. Peace is still relative but, because of the efforts of good people in both communities, sanity had triumphed.

There was in the minds of people on both sides of the community the fear that it could all go wrong again so easily. Months of patient searching had taught the Board of Governors and the Glenbryn residents that the path to suspension of a bitter protest is fraught with difficulties. We had got there by the goodness of people already mentioned but I am convinced that the prayers of untold numbers that we would find peace were a determining factor. People wrote promising prayers, sent pictures, rosaries, scapulars, and a multitude of other indications of their trust in the power of God to see us safely out of the awful situation the children and their parents had endured for far too long. On me personally it had a deep spiritual effect.

As I had on 2 September, the night before that first walk with the children and parents, so too on Sunday night, 25 November, I went into the monastery chapel. I wanted to say thanks to God for keeping everyone, on all sides, safe. And I also wanted to ask for a good outcome the next day as we tried to return to a more normal way of living together. Like many a 'cradle' Catholic I had grown up with prayer playing a part in my life. My training for Passionist life and priesthood had placed a strong emphasis on prayer. When I was a young student an attempt had been made to teach me to meditate and to pray. Only God can judge what success these efforts really had on me.

On Ardoyne Road, I learned a new way of praying. I learned that all prayer comes from the heart as much as from the head. The children and the parents taught me how love flows from one to the other. That must be how God's love also works. That is the key and the secret of prayer. I saw grown men crying out of sheer frustration that they could not rescue their child out of the monstrous thing that was happening. I could see God crying as (S)He watched her/his children on earth hate and kill each other.

The protestors also changed me beyond anything they may have imagined. One day, Christ said he was sorry for the crowd because they were like sheep without a shepherd. In no condescending way did I judge the protestors, but I would have loved to help bind up their wounds. They were raw and were hurting. They were lashing out in a way that was dangerous for all. They taught me how easy it is to fall out of love with your neighbour and how difficult it is to begin the long and arduous journey back to trust and tolerance. It may surprise the protestors to know that I prayed for them every day during the protest. It was not a case of just praying that it would end, but more a daily pleading with God that the hearts, spirits and minds of our Glenbryn neighbours would be touched by the power of God and healed of their wounds. These neighbours were part of my prayer life and taught me how to pray in a new way.

Even though the daily protest was suspended, much remained to be done. There were still large numbers of children in therapy and some remain so years afterwards. There were parents who were deeply hurt and angry about what had happened. Some remain so to this day. There was also much to be done in the school to build on the new-found peace and to consolidate all the good work that had been done during the months since term had begun. And there was still the daily uncertainty and worry that some incident might restart the horror that had just ended.

I had regular meetings with police to monitor the situation and see what could be done to resolve tensions before they led to breakdown. Holy Cross School opened an incident book that was to be faxed to the PSNI each Friday afternoon. In this way the fears and concerns of the parents could be examined and dealt with before the situation deteriorated.

This was my first Christmas at Holy Cross and I looked forward to it very much. Nativity plays in local schools, carol services in other schools, the preparation of cribs, Christmas trees in house windows – all went to build up an atmosphere of welcome and hope. There was a real chance that the peace of the first Christmas would come to Ardoyne and Glenbryn this year. It would be one of the best I could imagine. Most of all, the children would be safe and free from the dangers of past months.

The Midnight Mass was packed to the doors and the children of the parish were there in great numbers. That night, I took as the theme of the homily 'For to us a child is born.' (Isaiah 9:6). At that stage, I had been just over 150 days in Holy Cross and I confessed that night to the congregation that I had been reborn by the experiences on Ardoyne Road.

The Christmas holidays passed and, even though there had been no protest since the 23 November, there was apprehension as the return to school approached. New Year arrived and we welcomed in 2002, hoping and praying that better times lay ahead for all. Approximately 120 children had received counselling with the co-operation of their parents. As 2002 dawned, thirty children were still receiving counselling, both in groups and individually. In some instances, the school or the clergy heard of parents who had shown signs of trauma in the wake of the protest. Even now, in 2005, some parents when talking about the days of the protest will break into tears and sob.

An inter-agency group was set up in the school to monitor counselling and need in relation to trauma. Voluntary groups and statutory bodies had representatives as members. Despite this it would be wrong to think that everyone was in some form of crisis as 2002 began. Children who were particularly well behaved and hard working were rewarded regularly. Girl of the Week photographs were displayed in the entrance hall of the school. Peace maker stickers were given to children who were particularly kind and helpful at school or at home. Some great stories were told by the young pupils as they sincerely and seriously relayed their work to create peace and reconciliation!

However, there were also reminders that all was not finally settled. Electronic shutters and doors were fitted over all windows and doors in the school. Prior to the protest of 2001, the school had had some window shutters, as it had come under attack and been burned since opening in 1969. But now security was increased in a significant way. A security monitoring system of CCTV was installed to cover the buildings and grounds. At a later stage, this system had to be upgraded to capture images during the night following the throwing of pipe bombs into the school grounds.

As the preparations for the return to school in January 2002 continued, meetings with the police were held. It was agreed that every morning and afternoon, there would be a police patrol on Ardoyne Road as the children arrived and left. The parents and the governors were insistent on this as a way of keeping the fragile peace. In other places or situations, such precautions would seem excessive but here it was seen as absolutely necessary.

Somehow, we had 'limped' through December and had reached Christmas without major incidents. Monday, 7 January 2002, would be the real test. The parents and children made their way along Ardoyne Road that morning and arrived relieved that the journey had been without incident. There was still reluctance on the part of many to avail of the school buses.

As the week wore on, I began to believe that the worst was over. I was concerned by the occasional reports from some parents that words were exchanged as they walked to and from school, but there was nothing serious enough to consider that the protest was likely to begin again. In fairness, most people on both sides of the community were determined to maintain the peace.

Then, on Wednesday, 9 January, as I was walking towards Ardoyne Road to meet the parents and children as they returned in the afternoon I got a message that there was trouble. When I arrived a few minutes later, I could hardly believe my eyes. The return to something like normality, which had been developing, had totally collapsed. There was hand-to-hand fighting between parents and residents. Children were terrified and crying as stones and bottles began to fly. There was a complete breakdown of order. Cars outside the community house in Glenbryn where officials of the Northern Ireland Office were meeting had windows broken and damage done. Police immediately attempted to restore order, but it would be some days before anything resembling peace would return to Ardoyne.

Children and parents were now trapped in Holy Cross School as Ardoyne Road was totally blocked by the violence taking place. I phoned Anne Tanney at the School and she was already making arrangements for teachers and parents with cars, along with some taxis that had arrived, to evacuate the children. Once again, we relied on the goodness of St Gabriel's College to get the children and parents back home.

One of the difficulties was that some parents had been on their way to collect their children and so were not able to get to the school. It was understandable that they were frantic with worry for the safety of their children. All that could be done was to keep phone contact and relay as much information as possible. Again, great credit to the school and the community in that, within a short time, all the pupils were safely reunited with their parents.

The same scenario must have been played out for the parents and children of Wheatfield Primary School which is directly opposite Holy Cross School. Parents would have been arriving about the same time, with the same expectation of a quiet walk home with their little ones. And there was also worry about the safety of pupils coming from other schools who arrive back to Ardoyne or pass through it. Irrespective of the school or its denomination, there is no justification for putting in danger anyone who is simply going to and from school.

By the time I arrived on Ardoyne Road, I was already hearing an account of how the trouble had started. As with 19 June, there are various accounts of what happened that afternoon. Some of the local residents of Glenbryn spoke of the tearing down of a wreath marking the place where a resident had been killed. Parents assured me that one of them had been struck by a local resident and that the efforts of the police to make an arrest had been prevented by other residents.

Where a peace is as fragile as it was on Ardoyne Road, it was always the case that a breakdown could occur very easily. My own reaction was one of heartbreak that the tiny beginning so many people had made had been smashed to pieces. Within a very short time, rioting spread to other areas and spilled out onto the Crumlin Road. Beginning a riot may take little effort; it is extremely difficult to find a way to end it.

The police on the ground that afternoon immediately sought reinforcements. By the time darkness fell on that bleak early-January evening, there were 200 police on the streets of Ardoyne with a military back-up of 200 soldiers. The lines were set for a night of serious rioting and it was anybody's guess as to how long it would last or what the casualties would be.

Riots are a bit like a forest fire. They flare up in different areas and with varying degrees of intensity. It is not easy to predict where a riot will leap next. As night fell, petrol bombs, bricks and whatever was to hand was being thrown at the police lines. At least fourteen police officers were injured during hours of intense rioting. The police fired eight plastic baton rounds, and three young people were injured.

There are many arguments made about the use of 'plastic bullets'. There are safeguards now in that the Police Ombudsman examines afterwards any firing of them. With all that said, I consider it an abomination that any state authorises the firing of such lethal weapons. Death, blindness and serious injuries have resulted over the years of their use in Northern Ireland. They must be banned forever if we are to call ourselves a civilised society. Of course, the people – often young in age – who are involved in rioting should not be there. But when they are there, I have seen from first-hand experience that there are other ways of apprehending them or dispersing them. To resort to firing such lethal projectiles at unarmed people, mostly young, is never justified.

As the hours wore on, the rioting continued. Each time it seemed to be running out of steam, it resumed as intense as ever. There was the real danger that someone would be killed or seriously injured. As always in these situations, I felt completely helpless. Talks with the police yielded nothing. Talking with those involved in the throwing of missiles was equally unproductive. The best that could be done was to be there to help if needed.

At 2 a.m. on Thursday, the rioting was still continuing and, even though the numbers involved had reduced, it was clear that there was no will to give up and go home. However, an element of exhaustion was setting in and, eventually, an uneasy calm descended on the area. It was quite clear to me that this was nothing more than a lull in hostilities.

After the initial shock of seeing the mayhem on Ardoyne Road in the afternoon, once again the issue of closing the school the next day arose. Within the first hour of that afternoon, all the indications were that this was going to be a serious breakdown. My own wish would be to keep life as normal as possible for the children, even in the midst of so much chaos. They had done nothing to merit any disruption. This was an adult dispute over which they had no control. However, as always, there were some school governors not far away, and their advice was to close. It was, in many ways, the only responsible decision that could be made in the light of the intensity of what was happening. The teachers would be notified and we would use word of mouth to spread the message about the closure the next day. Members of the press also asked about this and so it soon became public knowledge that, once again, Holy Cross Girls' Primary School was in the eye of a storm.

Closing the school always felt to me, as chair of the governors, to be a failure. It was not a case of 'the show must go on', but a feeling of profound sorrow that children were being deprived of an education. However, once the decision was made, the main work was to see what could be done to halt the descent into further violence.

Thursday, 10 January, dawned to show the awful sight of what had happened in our midst. There was debris everywhere and the crunch of glass underfoot. These were the scars of the breakdown of trust and the suspicion that goes with it. Once again, the image of Ardoyne in particular, and North Belfast in general, that was shown around the world was one of hatred and violence. While there is no denying the evidence on the streets that morning, there is so much more of goodness and worth on every side of the community.

People are wonderfully resilient. On Thursday morning, people made their way to 7.30 a.m. and 10 a.m. Masses at Holy Cross. Staff arrived at the monastery and people in the locality got to work as best they could. Shops opened and people bought what they needed. Pupils went to schools in the locality that were open, and classes went ahead as normal. But it was still far from settled.

And worse was soon to come. At 11 a.m., a loyalist gang entered the grounds of Our Lady of Mercy Girls' Secondary School, not far from Holy Cross School. An armed man was put at the front door of the school, in which there were over 500 pupils. Nobody could enter or leave the building. Other members of the gang attacked and burned between seventeen and twenty cars parked in front of the school.

Pupils and teachers watched in horror as cars burned and fuel tanks exploded. The perpetrators of this cowardly act then left and were not seen again. Within a short while, fire brigades, police and emergency services arrived but nothing could be done other than to ensure that the fires did not spread.

Very quickly, news of this attack spread, and parents of these young pupils – at home, at work or on the streets – began frantic efforts to make contact. At this stage, it was not known if anyone had been injured. Fortunately, apart from the trauma of witnessing this appalling act, nobody was physically hurt. It was nothing short of a miracle that the school did not catch fire, with unimaginable consequences. The closing of Holy Cross Primary may have visited these events on the neighbouring Catholic School.

That evening, after darkness descended, disturbances flared again. The stand-off with the police and military was on again. The security forces came under attack from both sides of the community. That night, they fired seven baton rounds and arrests were made. Another night of intense violence followed.

All during the day, the question on many lips was about whether Holy Cross Girls' School would reopen on the Friday. Opinion was divided. Some felt that it would be far too dangerous to reopen, especially as the rioting showed little sign of abating. Others felt that if the school did not reopen, there could be huge pressure over the weekend not to open on the Monday.

The school governors were once again put in the unenviable position of having to make a decision that was fraught with difficulty. In the end, the decision was that the school would reopen on Friday and classes would run as normal. The bravery of the teachers and staff was once again being called upon as they were asked to trust in the governors' decision.

Thursday night was another late night as the disturbances continued unabated. The danger of serious injury or even death was never far away. By the early hours of Friday morning the worst seemed to have passed and it was possible to get to bed for a few hours of uneasy sleep.

Friday morning dawned to reveal once again the stark reality of the night before. The streets and footpaths resembled a battlefield. Once again, people made it to Mass, got the children ready for school, bought groceries and went about their business. Of course, everyone in the area was worried about the journey of the children along Ardoyne Road to Holy Cross School.

Appearances can be deceptive. Ardoyne Road was remarkably quiet considering the sustained violence of the previous two days and nights. Parents and children got to school and back home. It was a case of thanking God it was Friday. Even now, it is difficult to assess how much the young pupils knew of the apprehension their parents felt about the apparently simple task of going to school. Many of the children thought that they had had a special day off school the previous day. It was important not to add to their worries.

Then a sinister message was received. A group calling itself the Red Hand Defenders, a cover name previously used by the Ulster Defence Association, issued a death threat against all Catholic school-teachers and all other staff working in Catholic schools in North Belfast. No words can convey the shock waves that this caused. The situation had deteriorated to a depth not experienced before. 'Veterans' of the troubles would often say to me that I had seen nothing in comparison to 'the old days' of the late 1960s and the decades that followed. Some don't know that I was around Belfast in the early 1970s!

No longer was Holy Cross Girls' Primary School the only target. Now it was all teachers and all staff of every Catholic school – nursery, primary and secondary – in North Belfast. In the case of Holy Cross parish this had a profound effect. In surrounding parishes, the reaction was the same. When Bishop Donal McKeown called a meeting of school principals, teachers, staff and governors, it soon became clear how devastating this threat was proving to be.

My first reaction to such threats is not to over-react. It is almost a refusal to give people who would make such a despicable threat any attention. My heart went out to teachers and staff of Catholic schools of North Belfast who went to school leaving messages for loved ones in case they did not return. It was as serious as that.

With gratitude to God that no teacher, staff member or school governor had been killed, I went to bed on Friday night. I was in no way sure where we were in the efforts to return to normality. I awoke early on Saturday morning, 12 January, and listened to the early news. The first item was that a young postal worker had been shot dead. Danny McColgan, aged 20 years, arrived for work at a Royal Mail sorting depot at Rathcoole, County Antrim. The time was 4.45 a.m. and Danny was a Catholic, although that should not matter. However, because of his religion, he was shot dead. He left behind a baby daughter and his young partner. Loyalist paramilitaries had shot and killed him.

This was a chilling cold-blooded sectarian murder, and it led to further fear for all of us already under threat. Worse was to follow when all Catholic postal workers were put under death threat. Now, in the year 2002, we had a declared intention to kill teachers, school staff and postal workers for the sole reason that they were Catholics.

The trade unions and other groups were quick to react. A rally was called for the following Friday, 18 January, at various centres around Northern Ireland. Together with Fr Gary, I was present at City Hall, Belfast, to stand alongside all who were appalled and outraged by such blatant sectarianism. The speeches were powerful, the prayers were sincere and the presence of so many people of all ages and religions made a powerful statement. But it is sad to say that in some quarters sectarianism and its cousin, racism, are both alive and well.

On the Monday of that week, 14 January, Martin McGuinness, Minister for Education, had met with chief executives of educational groups to explore what could be done about the death threats hanging over the heads of teachers and schools' staff. There was a flurry of political activity. Statements were issued and there was a sense of horror that workers were being threatened on the basis of their religion.

The following day, the Shadow Northern Ireland Secretary, Quentin Davis, visited Holy Cross School once again. He offered his support and encouragement. The governors had been in contact with each other but met that afternoon in formal session. Part of the meeting was a session with Professor Brice Dickson, Chief Executive of the Northern Ireland Human Rights Commission, and some members of the Commission. It will be remembered that on a previous occasion Professor Dickson had been challenged by some of the parents for what appeared to be his reluctance to support the basic right of the children to access education without harassment. As has been mentioned, a parent had taken legal proceedings in November against John Reid, then Secretary of State, and the RUC. In the next chapter more will be said about this legal challenge and the role of Professor Dixon in the matter.

On Wednesday, 16 January an official of the Department of Foreign Affairs of the Irish Government came to Holy Cross to examine what had happened and to report to the minister responsible. That night, I was invited to have dinner in a Belfast restaurant with Richard Haas, US special envoy to Northern Ireland. The American Consul in Belfast, Barbara Stevenson, and some of her officials, and Rev John Dunlop of the Presbyterian Church were also present. Needless to say, the events of the previous week on Ardoyne Road were to the forefront of our conversation as the meal got under way.

Various opinions were expressed and reasons explored as to why violence had returned. I was impressed with Richard Haas and his grasp of the situation. He was absolutely clear that no cause could ever justify the damage done to young children, especially when all they were doing was trying to get to and from school.

The return to school in the New Year of 2002, which had started with so much hope and expectation, had quickly reminded all who cared to notice just how much remained to be done. The school governors were once again tested and found to be a tower of strength. Even with a death threat hanging over them, teachers, many of them young, came to school without complaint. They spent their days bringing comfort to their pupils and giving them an education and the hope of a better future. No words can possibly do justice to the bravery of these teachers and the staff of the schools. It would have been understandable if they had asked to have Catholics schools closed until the threat was lifted. Rather their response was to put their pupils first and put their own personal safety in second place. The damage done by evil people making threats is more than compensated for when you see bravery like this on the part of heroic men and women who will not bend in the face of personal danger. These teachers and staff will remain role models for me as long as I live. The parents appreciated this and the sad part is that we may not have had sufficient opportunities to express our admiration and appreciation.

CHAPTER TEN

ARDOYNE ROAD IS a short road. There are no twists or turns on it, but the events and their consequences in the early years of this millennium were far from straight-forward. People from all walks of life and outlooks got caught up in something they could never have imagined happening to them. Ordinary quiet people who wanted only to live in harmony with their neighbours were placed in a territory and environment never envisaged. I include myself among these people, as I had looked forward to my period in Ardoyne as being a quiet beginning to fast-approaching retirement – although the election of Pope Benedict XVI at 78 years of age may mean that I should revise my schedule!

Prior to 2001, the only time I had ever been in a court of law was to support my sister when she had to attend a court ruling on a rent review. That was all to change as the school protest intensified. Even without a legal background, it became clear to all who wanted to see that the law had failed to protect vulnerable children, all under 12 years of age. The state was allowing children to walk twice a day in immediate danger of serious injury and death. The fact that neither of these things happened is thanks to the protection of God and to the restraint and refusal to retaliate on the part of the parents and the wider community of Ardoyne.

Equally, many in the Glenbryn community could never have imagined that they would be seen all over the world in such a poor light. So many in that community did not deserve the condemnation visited on them because of the actions of some. As one elderly resident commented to me on Ardoyne Road after the protest was suspended, although she had lived all her adult life in Glenbryn, she would not have known many of those protesting outside her front door. She added that she felt so sorry for all of us as we went past morning, noon and afternoon. It is my certain knowledge that within the Glenbryn community there were some people who were heartbroken at what happened.

When faced with crimes against people of any sort, there is a temptation to expect others to do something about them. The need to address crimes and wrongdoing is not optional for anyone who hopes to find peace and reconciliation among people who have come to distrust and even despise each other. The Gospel of Jesus Christ places the pursuit and upholding of justice – in the sense of protecting the defenceless – as a central duty on all who would call themselves Christians. Indeed, all people of good will, even without the benefit of the Gospel, recoil at the sight of children being brutalised and damaged.

Originally I had offered to press for a judicial review on how the protest was policed and why the Secretary of State had allowed children to be put in mortal danger. However, even though I personally have no money or assets – I am not allowed have a bank account without supervision from the Passionist Congregation to which I belong – the property and other assets of the Passionists would disqualify me from obtaining legal aid. Moreover, my wish to make this application was not likely to succeed because no child (or grandchild) of mine was affected by the protest. No matter how intensely I or others felt about what happened to the children, we could not have been affected in the same way as a parent, guardian, sibling or other family member.

It was for these reasons that 'E', unemployed and at an address known only to the court swore under oath on 7 November that she 'together with all the children and most parents of children from this school, have been subjected to innumerable serious criminal offences, and breaches of our rights.' She described what parents and children had gone through since 19 June 2001 as 'inhuman and degrading treatment'.

Her sworn statement of the days from when the protest began on 19 June until the end of the school term in June makes harrowing reading even in the cold language of a court document. At the end of June, as the school closed for summer holidays, the hope was that a break of two months would give ample opportunity to find a resolution. But as we have already seen, this did not happen. 'E' describes the protest on 3 September 2001 as the new school term began as 'an even more violent and aggressive campaign against the children'.

'E' had been one of a number of parents who over the summer months had joined in dialogue with representatives of the protestors in search of a resolution. In her sworn statement, she says that 'it was clear that our efforts would prove fruitless after I received death threats from Loyalist paramilitaries, which I believe are a direct result of my being a parent and having engaged in this dialogue. On 5th September 2001 Sergeant B_____ called to my home to tell me that they had received a death threat that I would be executed on sight.'

The police indicated to her that the threat and others received subsequently came from the Red Hand Defenders. Taking these threats seriously, she and her family moved out of the family home in Ardoyne into temporary accommodation.

In a further affidavit, made on 16 November 2001, 'E' refers to the change in policing the protest on Ardoyne Road. Her summary is that 'it remains the case that the conditions under which I bring my child to and from Holy Cross School remain frightening and intimidating, despite the improvements.' The greatest concern for her was 'the increasing proximity of protestors to myself and other parents and children when walking to and from Holy Cross School'.

Her belief was that the police were taking a 'softly softly' approach with the protestors in contrast to a more heavy-handed way of dealing with the parents. She gives an example under oath that a few days earlier she was walking on the footpath with her daughter to school. She was stopped by two men who stood in front of her, spat at her and used abusive language towards her. They told her to go back onto the roadway where she belonged. She recounts how police appeared at once and ushered her off the footpath and onto the road while the two men remained on the footpath.

A whole book would be needed to capture the extent of the stories told in the affidavits made both during and after the protest. Affidavits were made by others such as Anne Tanney, the school principal, Fr Gary, Terry Laverty, principal of Holy Cross Boys' School and a school governor, a local medical doctor who told of many consultations with young patients who were pupils at the school. Other brave and courageous people raised their voices in defence of the children and their rights. Reading through each of these accounts brings back something of the reality of what was happening. As already mentioned, I had missed many of the details because I had chosen to focus solely on the children in their daily struggle to get to and from school.

It is also clear that these affidavits are not 'sectarian' diatribes but the honest retelling of what happened to 225 children over a period of months. The evidence of the media reports and pictures had already made the story known around the world. It is interesting to feed 'Holy Cross' into a computer search engine and find the thousands of references that are shown. An attempt was now being pursued to hold the state accountable. The recollections being collected and sworn as true were not for publication but as evidence in pursuit of truth and justice.

My own affidavits tell as honestly as I could what I saw, and what happened to those of us who walked Ardoyne Road from 3 September until 23 November 2001. I could not comment on the events that unfolded in June 2001 as I was still living in Italy. The most recent affidavit I made was in 2004 to counter the opinion of the state that the matter of the Holy Cross protest was of academic interest only. Unfortunately, this was not the case as will be seen in the next chapter.

In addition to the people listed above, affidavits were made by police officers and members of the Northern Ireland Human Rights Commission. While all affidavits sworn were of great value, an important insight is gained by the perspective offered by people from these two groups. A number of police officers made affidavits recounting their side of the story. Chief Superintendent Roger Maxwell was the District Commander at the time of the protest. He had overall responsibility for policing in the North Belfast area. It was his claim that the police throughout the dispute sought to facilitate safe passage for the pupils and their parents to and from school each day. There is no disagreeing with this statement and I have no doubt that this was the intention. In writing to Chief Superintendent Maxwell on 22 November 2001, the day before the protest was suspended, I said: 'I wish to record here my appreciation for the manner in which you and your colleagues have received my questions and suggestions.' Then I added: 'We have not always agreed on all matters, but your interest and concern were evident.'

What we could never have agreed on was the length of time the children were left in mortal danger and the number of times our questions and objections were replied to in terms of 'right to protest' by those targeting small children on Ardoyne Road. It always seemed to me and to others that the children and the protestors were seen by police as equal participants in some kind of a show of strength. They seemed to miss the fact that we were seeing a daily abuse of children by adults who claimed not to be targeting them.

It still amazes me that court records would subsequently show that Chief Superintendent Maxwell believed that more aggressive police tactics would undoubtedly have led to even more serious public disorder and 'the probable involvement of loyalist paramilitary organisations' and 'the lives of parents and children would have been imperilled if this had happened'.

Over the months of the protest, I came to respect Chief Superintendent Maxwell and found him to be unfailingly courteous. But it is beyond belief that he could speak of the 'probable' involvement of paramilitaries. Equally, we already had death threats, a bomb, daily uncertainty as to what would happen next, and so it is difficult to know whether more robust policing could have made things any worse than they already were.

At the time of the protest Alan McQuillan was Assistant Chief Constable and, among other duties, he was responsible for monitoring the performance of District Commanders, including Maxwell.

Assistant Chief Constable McQuillan made two sworn affidavits in which he also affirmed that the overriding concern of the police was the safety of the parents and children. He went on to deal with the 'real risk' of serious violence elsewhere and the risk of attacks on Catholic schools that might be sparked had the protest been handled in a different way.

Alan McQuillan rightly pointed out that the only true and lasting solution lay in dialogue between all sectors of the community in this area of North Belfast. He assured the court in his statements that the police were alert to the rights of the children and their parents arising under Articles 2 and 3 of the European Convention on Human Rights and Fundamental Freedoms. From a police perspective, the 'real risk' may have been elsewhere. For parents, families, neighbours, parishioners and school governors, there was one immediate 'real risk' and that was present in the daily danger to Mary, Róisín and other real little children.

During the revelations of the child abuse issues in the Catholic Church around the world, many commentators spoke of a 'clerical culture'. In this way of looking at things, the starting point is the institution and not the survivor who is often a child cruelly abused by a priest or religious. In the same way, I came to see that there is also a 'police culture'. In one of his affidavits, Assistant Chief Constable McQuillan describes the policing of the protest as 'both fair and professional, respecting and balancing the rights of all those involved.'

A parent, a brother or sister, a relative, or a priest walking with the children could never speak of respecting and balancing of rights. Only a police officer could use language like this. There was no balancing of the rights of people who daily abused and threatened the lives and health of small girls, with the rights of those small girls, and certainly no respecting of the rights of the children. If this is what policing is about, we all have to be greatly concerned for the most vulnerable in our society. Other officers of the RUC who were involved in policing the protest made similar points to those of Chief Superintendent Maxwell and Assistant Chief Constable McQuillan.

In all my dealing with ACC McQuillan I found him to be always ready to take a phone call, even when at home, to deal with urgent matters. On that level, I could not speak highly enough of the conduct and courtesy of those police officers with whom I had contact from my arrival at Holy Cross in late July 2001.

At the time of the Holy Cross School protest, Sir Ronnie Flanagan was Chief Constable and he was obviously a key person in all that happened. I spoke to him on only one occasion when he was in a police helicopter over Ardoyne during a particularly difficult situation. I never had an opportunity to meet with him during the months of the protest. His direction of policing was conveyed through the officers on the ground in North Belfast. An area of dispute in pursuing the judicial review arose because of differences between the Chief Constable, Ronnie Flanagan, and the Northern Ireland Human Rights Commission (NIHRC). On 6 September 2001, three days after the children returned to school, a delegation from the NIHRC met with the Chief Constable.

One of the Human Rights Commissioners claimed in his affidavit that when he asked if the Chief Constable would walk his own child up Ardoyne Road, the Chief Constable replied that he would and, further, that he would expect the police to 'facilitate' him. This Commissioner recalled the Chief Constable saying that the protest was a 'black and white public order issue'.

Yet in a replying affidavit on 21 January 2002, Sir Ronnie Flanagan says that he did not say that the Holy Cross protest was a 'black and white public order issue'. What he claims he said was that he 'saw the issue of children being able to go to their school unmolested as a straight forward "black and white issue".' In other words, he says it was more than a public order issue. The Chief Constable also challenged other parts of the affidavit from this Human Rights Commissioner. For instance, he revealed that he personally would not walk a child of his along Ardoyne Road in the circumstances then prevailing. He would, however, expect the police to make the choice of so doing available to him.

Another meeting took place between the NIHRC and the Chief Constable on 25 October 2001. The same Commissioner mentioned above put in his sworn affidavit that his recollection of the meeting was that the Chief Constable conceded that in organising the policing on Ardoyne Road they had failed to take into account the best interests of the children. But this was later disputed by the Chief Constable in his January 2002 affidavit. He claimed to have emphasised during the meeting that everything that was being done by the police 'was driven by what was in the best interests of the children'.

To substantiate his claim, he referred to correspondence in November 2001 between himself and Professor Brice Dickson, Chief Commissioner, in which he wrote to the effect that 'the rights of the children are to the forefront of our thinking in all that we do and all we are seeking to achieve.'

The worrying part of all of this is that the original comments of the Human Rights Commissioner were supported by another two Commissioners who also attended the meeting and who had both walked Ardoyne Road with the children. Some very moving and detailed testimonies were given by individual Commissioners who walked with the children and parents.

One Commissioner spoke of finding her walk down Ardoyne Road both intimidating and stressful. She described it as like a walk through a highly militarised tunnel while under the fear of verbal and physical attack. She concluded that the effect on children who had to undertake this walk twice every day would be 'catastrophic'. Then she gives a reflection making a connection with her own family and the experience of a child starting school:

> My middle child started school on the same day as the Holy Cross school started back and the protest recommenced. She is a very confident child and was very excited about starting the school where her older sister already attends. As it came to her first day I had the natural anxiety of all parents, in particular I was hoping that she would not have her confidence knocked early on and that her time at school would be as good as her high expectations of it. As a parent I felt that an unfortunate incident in the early days could taint her view of school, and consequently her education, forever. These were my fears sending my own child to school in a peaceful area and with no reason to believe that there would be a negative experience. I cannot therefore imagine the effect on children whose only experience of school is going through this

protest, or even without this trip, who attend a school where a feeling of basic security is missing.

This is a long quote from a sworn affidavit but it gives as good an insight as I have read of what only a parent of a small child can know. The reactions of the Commissioners who visited the school and walked Ardoyne Road reveal a deep disquiet with what they found. Indeed, two Commissioners undertook to be present on Ardoyne Road on a daily basis, so moved were they by what was happening.

The Chief Commissioner, Professor Brice Dickson, made a decision not to walk with the children but to meet parents, children and governors both on Ardoyne Road and at the school. On one such visit to Ardoyne Road, he was filmed being criticised by parents for refusing to walk all the way with them to the school. He emerged from behind the military vehicles and it appeared as though he had been visiting the protestors.

This was an embarrassing incident for the NIHRC, and the members struggled to know how to respond to this incident. Some in the Commission appear to have felt that their function was simply to explain the rights of all involved. There were, fortunately, others who wanted the Commission to take a more proactive role. These latter voices wanted the Commission to be seen as strongly endorsing the rights of children as paramount in this situation.

There were now clear divisions within the Commission and this issue continues to haunt the NIHRC to this day. Rather than the divisions being just a negative, though, good was to come out of the convictions of those Commissioners who were not prepared to keep quiet and go with the leadership. On 24 October 2001, the Casework Committee of the NIHRC called an emergency meeting to discuss whether the Commission should take a case in its own name against the police and/or the Secretary of State that proper policing had not been employed.

To its credit, the Casework Committee voted in favour of a case being taken. It was felt that the Commission as a whole was the appropriate place to debate this decision. Legal advice was sought from senior counsel and a heated debate took place on 26 October 2001.

On 5 November 2001, a meeting was called of the Casework Committee to discuss as a matter of urgency a request from a parent ('E') who wanted to take a case as already outlined. This committee agreed to do this, but at a full meeting of the Commission one week later some Commissioners expressed reservations about the decision to support 'E' in her legal action. Then the situation became complicated. Professor Brice Dickson made public on 19 November the notes he had of the meeting held on 25 October with Sir Ronnie Flannagan. The RUC Chief Constable telephoned Brice Dickson to express his concerns that the Commission was supporting 'E' and that it was doing so without informing him of the decision. Further, he was concerned that notes of the meeting of 25 October had been released as evidence to support 'E' in her claim.

The cracks now began to become wider and more public. The Human Rights Commission met again on 26 and 27 November. On 4 December, Brice Dickson wrote to Ronnie Flannagan indicating that at least three Human Rights Commissioners were not happy with the decision to support the case being taken. There are also indications that some Human Rights Commissioners were unhappy that some of their colleagues on the NIHRC were swearing affidavits on behalf of 'E' and sending to the High Court the Commission's notes of its meeting on 25 October with the Chief Constable.

In his letter to the Chief Constable, Brice Dickson added that he did not think the police action in connection with Holy Cross School protest amounted to a breach of the Human Rights Act. This was written on official Commission headed paper, in respect of a case that the Commission was itself supporting. It is tempting to say that we had reached an 'Alice in Wonderland' situation.

Meanwhile, as Christmas came and went, the suffering of the children at Holy Cross Girls' Primary School had not finished. Remember that by this stage between 50 and 60 per cent of these young girls had gone into counselling. In June 2002, there were still over thirty of these children receiving therapy. Yet within the NIHRC and within the RUC, there were arguments going on about whether things were really that bad for these little ones, and there were those who apparently saw very little wrong with the fact that they had been subjected to constant trauma from June to November 2001.

In March 2002, the Chief Constable, in a letter to Brice Dickson, asked the NIHRC to reconsider its funding of the case being taken by 'E'. It was suggested that if the funding for the case were not withdrawn, Professor Dickson's letter to the Chief Constable, disagreeing with the support given by the Commission, would be made public in court.

The 'horse trading' going on at the highest level in the RUC and the NIHRC may surprise some and may merely confirm the suspicions of others. Within any organisation, there are agendas held to be of fundamental importance. Surely in this case, the sight of the children on their daily walk to and from school had a more fundamental right to priority than any 'point scoring'.

Eventually, in April 2002, the correspondence between the two leaders of these organisations became public. The establishment of the Human Rights Commission as part of the 1998 Good Friday Agreement was a real sign of hope. It is as necessary as ever but it will take some time for it to recover from its involvement in the Holy Cross School judicial review, in spite of those wonderfully courageous Commissioners who left the safety of their office desks and saw for themselves what the violation of rights looks like.

On 31 October 2001, a meeting took place between Jane Kennedy, Security Minister at Stormont, and members of the Human Rights Commission. One of the Commissioners present raised the issue of the proximity of the protestors to the parents and children. This was particularly worrying given that there had been two bomb attacks, one injuring a police officer and the other injuring a soldier. Referring to the bomb attack of 5 September 2001 on Ardoyne Road, RUC Chief Constable Flanagan, in his 21 January 2002 affidavit, says that he has 'no doubt that this attack was against police officers who were moving a crowd to make a safe passage for the children and their parents who wanted to walk to Holy Cross School.' This does not match what I witnessed that morning which was an attack on children walking to school. As stated earlier, it was totally regrettable that an officer and a dog were hurt.

At the meeting, it was put to Minister Kennedy that posters

naming Aidan Troy as a paedophile priest were to be clearly seen on Ardoyne Road. Her response was that, as far as she was aware, the posters were not on display every day. I don't want to comment too much on this, but it strikes me as amazing that the implication of the Minister's reply was that occasional defamation is all right as long as it is not repeated every day for almost three months. This branding would lead eventually to a more sinister attack. As recently as April 2005 I was surrounded by a group of people while visiting in the Mater Hospital, Belfast. These people verbally abused me publicly as 'a sectarian priest'. Decency forces me to omit a few words from what I have quoted them as saying.

While the children and their parents were trudging up and down Ardoyne Road, a war of words broke out between Security Minister Jane Kennedy and Brice Dickson. In essence, she was upset that a Human Rights Commissioner had used notes taken at the meeting with her, in his affidavit in support of the case being taken by 'E'. Jane Kennedy wrote to Brice Dickson stating her upset in no uncertain terms. Brice Dickson wrote back with an explanation that bordered on an apology. Again, these 'behind the scenes' moves contributed nothing to relieving the anguish of the children or parents but merely showed how remote people can become from where the real hurt is being inflicted.

There were many delays and obstacles to be overcome. A chronology of exactly how much resistance there was to this action being taken will have to wait for another book. Suffice it to say that, with delays behind us and different obstacles overcome, the case of 'E' was heard before Mr Justice Brian Kerr in Belfast. I sat on the hard benches of the courthouse to listen to the arguments put forward for and against the action.

Queen's Counsel for 'E' contended that the policing operation had failed to protect adequately the rights of the children and parents arising under various articles of the European Convention on Human Rights and Fundamental Freedoms. It was suggested that the police approach should have been informed by the United Nations Convention on the Rights of the Child.

Counsel put forward the view that the police strategy was

fundamentally flawed in that it dealt with the protest in a manner appropriate to a contentious parade, rather than analysing the requirements for the protection of the human rights of the children and their parents. 'The best interests of the child' as a guiding principle did not inform police strategy.

It was strange to sit in court over a number of days and hear what I and others had sworn being quoted to the judges. There were times when I would have loved to stand up and make some point in support of the truth of what happened, but I quickly learned that once an issue gets into the courts, it takes on a life of its own. Sometimes I wonder if the truth of what actually happened has to give way to whichever counsel comes up with the stronger legal points and argument.

Naturally, a defence of the actions of the Chief Constable and the Secretary of State followed. Arguments were made against there having been any violation of the applicant's rights and much of this part of the hearing was quite technical. It was difficult to sit and listen to the defence counsel say that the police were obliged to be alert to the potential rights of the protestors under Articles 10 and 11 of the Convention. While it was admitted that much of the conduct of the protestors could not be justified, it was deemed 'simplistic' to suggest that no balancing exercise was required.

When I was a student for the priesthood, I once won a prize at end-of-term examinations in the seminary, for excellence at Canon Law. This is the law that governs the Catholic Church from a legal perspective. At that stage, in the late 1960s I even considered whether I might follow a legal career from within the priesthood. I never did and my experiences to date have made me glad that I didn't.

The judgement of the court was delivered on 17 June 2004. It was acknowledged that 'the actions of many who engaged in this protest were disgraceful. The intimidating, threatening and oppressive behaviour of several of the protestors towards innocent children and their parents were indefensible.' The judge further ruled the he 'simply cannot accept that it has been proved that the authorities knew or ought to have known at the time of the existence of a real and immediate risk to the applicant's life'. To me, this is amazing.

In the judgment handed down in June 2004, three years after the protest began, the point is made that 'there is an understandable inclination to view the matter of policing in straightforward terms'. There follows an accurate description of what happened and the judgment ends up by saying that the reaction to the protestors might be that 'they should have been prevented from doing so; they should have been arrested and prosecuted'.

A most extraordinary statement, at least in my estimation, follows: 'Sadly, policing options and decisions do not readily permit such uncomplicated solutions, particularly in such a uniquely fraught situation.' The following comment could be written only by one who had not set foot on Ardoyne Road to experience this 'uniquely fraught situation': 'Those who had to decide how to deal with this protest were obliged to have regard to the effect that their decisions might have in the wider community.'

It was all right to let the children suffer rather than risk violence in the wider community. I wonder why the phrase 'sacrificial lambs' comes to my mind. Then the police are handed almost carte blanche: 'It is precisely because the Police Service is better equipped to appreciate and evaluate the dangers of such secondary protests and disturbances that an area of discretionary judgment must be allowed them, particularly in the realm of operational decisions.'

Reading the above, I thanked God that I am a priest and not a legal person. When I think of how Jesus made the child the model of the Kingdom he came to establish, and how he warned about hurting one of these little ones, it becomes clear that the higher court of God's law has more to offer. The parents of those who suffered so intensely may have judgments delivered against them in earthly courts but in the Court of Heaven the verdict is in their favour.

More disturbing words followed in the judgement when it was stated that 'the possible rights of the protestors under Articles 10 (freedom of thought, conscience and religion) and 11 (freedom of expression) of the Convention could not simply be ignored by the police.'

It is worth quoting the last paragraph of the June 2004 judgment in full:

The sense of outrage that these events provoked cannot be allowed to substitute for a dispassionate and scrupulous examination of the legality of the policing strategy and the decisions taken as to how the protest should be handled, however. That appraisal must take place with a well-defined legal framework.

Having conducted that assessment, I have concluded that the policing judgments made have withstood the challenge that has been presented to them. The application for judicial review must be dismissed.'

The judge may have dismissed the judicial review but that is not the end of the story. An appeal has been lodged and legal aid obtained. I have met with 'E' and she is determined to go ahead. After legal arguments, most of which I did not understand, the appeal is going ahead and will eventually be heard. It is my conviction that if justice and truth mean anything, it is not possible to walk away from this testing of the matter through the courts.

Some have thought that this is some sort of revenge against the people of Glenbryn. Nothing could be further from the truth. The protestors were not helped by the decisions made by the Secretary of State and the police. Had matters been handled differently it is likely that the damage done to the reputation of the Glenbryn community would have been greatly reduced.

If the judicial review appeal fails, I hope that we can take the matter to the House of Lords at Westminster. If that fails, we will have to go to the European Court of Human Rights. This is not a campaign for revenge any more than the walk to school was a parade.

It is generally agreed that the NIHRC involvement in the Holy Cross court case proved to be a disaster. It gives me no joy to agree with that assessment. As stated previously, one of the positive elements to emerge was the courage displayed by some Human Rights Commissioners in becoming involved on the ground when many other organisations decided it was safer to stay away. One of them, as already mentioned, paid the price of his losing a most prestigious job because of his commitment. It is doubtful if the Holy Cross dispute caused the divisions within the Commission that lead to resignations. It is more likely that those divisions existed already and, as time went on, were magnified.

In an interview on 4 April 2003, Chief Commissioner Brice Dickson is quoted as saying that 'the reality was that we were too small and too unimportant an organisation to achieve very much.' His humility is admirable but he fails to realise that there were so few bodies to reduce the loneliness of Ardoyne Road during those awful days and months. This could have been the making of the NIHRC and could really have put it on the map, rather than showing it in such a poor light.

I now know that, in my declining years, rather than studying law, I would love to do some studies and work in the area of human rights, especially as they affect children and families. Apart from anything else, this lies at the heart of the Gospel.

It should be remembered that during this time the children and parents were still uncertain that normality had definitely returned. The events of January 2002 had been a reminder of just how fragile the peace still was and how easy it would be for a rapid fall into violence once again.

A new 'brush' with the courts was not far away. By summer, a proposal to build a wall across Ardoyne Road had surfaced once again. This was sincerely put forward by the residents of Glenbryn in response to ongoing violence in the area. While not calling into question the sincerity of the request for this form of protection, it became urgent that this be stopped. If it were not stopped, the day the wall was constructed, even though it would have a gate built into it, Holy Cross Girls' Primary School would have to close. The next chapter examines the issues involved.

CHAPTER ELEVEN

WHEN PEOPLE ARE suspicious of each other or afraid of what might happen, a wall can look like a solution. In Belfast and throughout Northern Ireland over the years of the Troubles, 'peace walls' have sprouted up and show no sign of going away. In Jerusalem, a wall is being built by Israel to keep Palestinians at arm's length. Berlin had a famous wall until it eventually came down and a divided city could once again breathe with two lungs. In Ardoyne, there is a dividing wall between loyalist Glenbryn and nationalist Ardoyne. It has been strengthened and heightened over the past few years. While the past two summers have seen relatively little violence in the area, there is always the stark reminder that all is not well.

There are fewer bridges in Belfast than walls. Not only are the bridges across the Lagan few in number, but so too are the bridges between people of differing outlooks and cultures. To build a bridge is far more demanding than to build a wall. For a bridge to reach others, you need courage and not concrete, strength rather than stones. But it is so difficult to find the starting point for the bridge and often the foundations give way after even the best of efforts.

At the suspension of the protest, there was a huge sense of relief but very little trust. Some residents of Glenbryn still came to the shops at Ardoyne and collected pensions. There was an absence of daily violence, but not a presence of peace. People were still afraid. With fear in the air, it is immensely difficult to start rebuilding community trust and good relationships.

On 28 November 2001, the Office of the First and Deputy First Minister wrote to me offering assistance in the formation of a Joint Community Forum for Ardoyne and Upper Ardoyne. This forum was to agree its own procedures and meeting schedule. A draft memorandum of understanding and procedure had already been prepared by their Office.

More was to follow. On 30 November 2001 the Office of the First and Deputy First Minister along with the Department of Social Development, invited me to the launch of the North Belfast Community Action Project. The launch was to take place on Monday, 3 December, in Belfast. The leader of the project had already been selected, Very Rev. John Dunlop. There were elaborate procedures outlined by which his two assistants would be selected. In the end, the other two selected were Roy Adams, CEO of Building Design Partnership and Monsignor Tom Toner of St Peter's Cathedral. Never did I see a group of people work harder and end up with so little achieved.

The Project's vision was to create a vibrant and sustainable community in North Belfast that would be influential in supporting peace-building. The buzz word of their work became 'building community capacity'. It was held as incontestable that the root problem of the Holy Cross School protest arose from a lack of capacity, real or imagined, within loyalist communities. It would be as unkind as it would be unfair to deny that lack of capacity is a factor on both sides of the divide. But to hold as axiomatic that the creation of more capacity on the Loyalist side of the divide would eliminate all problems is simply not tenable.

The project sought to focus on producing early outcomes and practical assistance to local communities. One of the problems was that the people examining the issues were not living in the local community affected. As noted before, there were so many people working on the ground who could have written the report in half the time, with half the cost, because the issues were their 'bread and butter' of everyday life. As was the case during the protest, there was a lack of urgency about reaching the deep hurts that to this day afflict both sides of the divide. The Project sought to treat the surface scars but never reached the wounds.

There was a claim made that while it would be resourced and supported by government it would be independent of government. A nod to local involvement was in the hope that the work would be underpinned by independent action conducted by researchers and community workers who would have experience of working in divided communities.

When the report of the Project Team was published in May 2002, it was clear that a huge amount of time, effort and money had gone into reaching that point. It was then that the project hit the buffers and went no further. The report was presented to First Minister, David Trimble and Deputy First Minister Mark Durkan and local MP Nigel Dodds on 29 May. The kernel of the report is to be found in the section entitled 'Recommended Further Action'. With all due respect I or a child walking up and down Ardoyne Road during the protest could have come up with the same conclusions:

- enable Government to respond in a more 'joined up' way
- address interface issues
- boost community capacity
- improve the economic, social and cultural life in North Belfast
- improve health and education in the area.

The report goes on to make nine specific recommendations which include £15 million additional funding over five years with support for extra funding for both health and education. There is no denying that the aspirations were right and obvious. However, it is sad to note that in mid-2005, savage health and education cuts have had devastating effects everywhere, but particularly in North Belfast. Strikes in protest against education cuts and the sad spectacle of patients on trolleys continue unabated. It has been my sad experience to spend days trying to get a young person into medical care when his or her life was in danger.

The parents of one young man who took his own life had been seen by a member of the health service the afternoon before. He had been promised an appointment for psychiatric assessment for some distant date. The pain was too great and he could not wait. For a suicidal person, to wait four or five hours in an Accident and Emergency department is not acceptable.

Among the more unusual recommendations in the report was mention of a 'Centre for Citizenship' and a 'Music Action Zone', along with e-technology for 'non-confrontational' communication. Several years later, the housing waiting list is still a scandal. Because of education cuts, teachers are being made redundant and the funding of worthwhile community projects is a constant headache.

There is no denying that sincere efforts were made by some to address the aftermath of the Holy Cross School protest, but the feeling was abroad that this was a cosmetic exercise on the part of government. There was also the danger of a false hope being given that something would happen which would make a real difference. Most people who had come through the protest knew that the report would gather dust before it gathered momentum.

If the North Belfast Community Action Project was something of a damp squib, the next proposal from the government was of a far more serious and real nature. It was, in fact, a re-emergence of the proposal to build a wall across Ardoyne Road, but, of course, it was never stated like that. Language such as realignment of the road and redesign were the less threatening words employed.

Commencement on the works promised in the document that had led to the suspension of the school blockade came about slowly. It was good to see that the issues of the Glenbryn residents regarding feeling unsafe in their homes were being addressed. It is to nobody's advantage to be afraid of injury or attack in your own home. By 25 January 2002 the Office of the First and Deputy First Minister could report that the ramps on Ardoyne Road were completed.

But all was not moving smoothly. By mid-January, a first design for altering the Alliance Avenue/Ardoyne Road intersection was in progress. The politicians were quite explicit in a letter sent to me in which they said, 'This design, on which the Concerned Residents of Upper Ardoyne were very actively engaged, now fully reflects the wishes of the people of Upper Ardoyne.' In other words, the plans for the alteration to the road where the protest had been staged was given over to the protesting community without at that stage any consultation with the parents, the school, the Board of Governors or the people of Ardoyne.

I can remember a meeting weeks later in which we begged the beleaguered lady from Groundwork NI, who was part of the design team, simply to give us a clean sheet of paper and let us start all over again. We were put in the position of children sitting an examination – we were given a design and told to comment. We were not free to reject the design but could only comment on what we liked or wished to alter.

Underlying all of this was a belief on the part of the parents and the community generally in Ardoyne that a verbal agreement had been given to the protestors in November that a wall would be built across Ardoyne Road. As part of that wall, a gate would be included, and the key would be given to the residents of Glenbryn who would be in charge of opening and closing it. The name of an aide of a leading Unionist politician was given to me as the one who had given the assurance.

On 23 January 2002, a news item in the *Irish News* newspaper indicated that the building of a wall across Ardoyne Road would be going ahead. This had a serious effect on Holy Cross School so soon after the suspension of the protest. The enrolment was already falling as, understandably, parents weighed up carefully if it was prudent to enrol a girl not yet four years of age in a school that was having a wall built on the road leading to it. Who could blame them?

That same day, I got a letter from Security Minister Jane Kennedy. Her letter dealt with security matters, as they are still reserved to the control of the government at Westminster. In her letter she says, 'Could I take this opportunity to mention the story carried in the *Irish News* today and to confirm that the Chief Constable has *not* [her emphasis] made any recommendation to build a wall across the Ardoyne Road nor have I considered any such proposal. In the report the Chief Constable confirms that he does not recommend the installation of a security gate.'

The words of the Security Minister are clear as is her quoting of the Chief Constable. Yet the construction of a roundabout or wall remained on the agenda of the Office of the First and Deputy First Minister for the next number of months. Right up to summer 2002, various ways were sought to bring the people of Ardoyne on board. I shudder to think how much money was spent in trying to achieve the impossible.

As late as 23 August 2003, I received a letter from David Trimble and Mark Durkan, acknowledging the 'series of meetings and correspondence with you during May and June'. On 28 June, the First and Deputy First Ministers appointed independent arbitrators 'to address remaining issues on community safety'. At once, it became clear that there was an element of panic taking hold. The marching season was in full swing, and the tension in Ardoyne was high with the 12 July marches just over two weeks away. Added to this was the fact that it is the practice of many nationalists to go on holidays for the '12th fortnight'.

David Trimble and Mark Durkan in their letter indicated that they 'had accepted the three recommendations' of the arbitrators' report. Already, they 'are now examining how best to implement all of the recommendations as quickly as possible.' It was their intention 'to bring the report to the Executive in order to secure agreement on the proposed way forward.'

Recommendation 1 of the Arbitrators' Report was to construct a wall, 3 metres high, from the top of Alliance Avenue onto the front of the Glenbryn houses. Where the wall was to end, a 3-metre fence would continue up part of Ardoyne Road. The other two proposals were about confidence building, dialogue and a process to be devised to test consensus on further improvements.

Had it not been so serious and really a matter of life and death for both sides of the community, it would have been funny. Back in January, there had been an underlined assurance by the Security Minister that the Chief Constable had *not* made a decision to build a wall, and now in August we had the wall not only proposed, but about to be built.

There were many meetings within Ardoyne to look at what might be done to ensure the security of the Glenbryn residents, while maintaining a clear view all along Ardoyne Road as far as Holy Cross

School. The parents at meetings made it quite clear that if the wall was built, they would not have the confidence to send their children to school. A wall can be good for security but it can also be used as a hiding place in an attack. This can apply to both sides of the wall. Even if there has never been an attack, there is always the fear that one day it might happen.

If the proposals to build a wall had come from both sides of the Ardoyne community, it would have been possible to find a compromise design. But the call for a wall had the potential to reignite the protest. Traffic calming was seen as non-controversial. Better housing was a matter for the residents and the authorities involved. The strengthening of the 'peace wall' between Alliance Avenue and Glenbryn, as well as a CCTV camera, were accepted as helping everyone in some way.

As has been stated, had the wall been built, it would have been necessary to close the school. Such an outcome would not only have been a terrible blow for the parish of Holy Cross but would also have focused world attention on the Glenbryn community once again. From the moment the protest was suspended, the aim of all people had to be to move forward and create a better future for everyone.

Meetings locally and at Stormont failed to resolve the issues dividing us. One of the meetings the Board of Governors attended at the request of David Trimble was to take place at 3.30 p.m. on Wednesday, 1 May 2002, at Stormont. The group of governors arrived shortly after 3 p.m. and, once we had security clearance, I notified an official of our presence for the meeting. We were asked to wait and were told that we would be called. We waited and we waited but the call never came. When 4 p.m. came and went and still no call or any information on what was happening it was agreed among the governors that we would leave and go home. This we did.

Just before 5 p.m., I had begun visiting some parishioners when I received a phone call from a somewhat agitated official in Stormont who asked where I and the other governors were. Not being able to speak for the others, I replied that I was doing some pastoral visitation in Holy Cross parish. The agitated voice on the phone asked if I did not know that a meeting had been arranged with the First and Deputy

First Ministers. I pointed out that we had waited almost one hour for this meeting without receiving any information.

She asked if it would be possible for me to round up the other governors and get back to Stormont immediately as the Ministers were waiting for us. This was out of the question. The next suggestion was that I gather the governors together and the Ministers would meet us that evening in Holy Cross Monastery. I promised to do the best I could, and the time was set for 8.30 p.m. The other governors were interested in the prospect of David Trimble, Mark Durkan and their officials holding a meeting in Ardoyne, and in the monastery at that!

From around 8 p.m. onwards, I started to get updates as regards the progress of the Stormont delegation as it made its way to Ardoyne. There was going to be no repeat of what happened earlier in the evening. The delegation arrived minus David Trimble but with an Ulster Unionist politician in his place. I was at the monastery door to welcome with a handshake each member of the Stormont delegation. In many ways, this was a historic moment in the 133-year existence of Holy Cross Monastery.

The meeting got under way about 9 p.m. and every aspect of the implementation of the measures on Ardoyne Road was examined and discussed. At one stage, David McNarry, then an advisor to the First Minister, strongly indicated that we as governors should show some gratitude to Mr Trimble for all the time, attention and hard work he had put into these matters. To me it was extraordinary to hear the governors being lectured about our need to be grateful. It almost seemed that the school was being held responsible for the events between 19 June and 23 November.

In the face of such unfair treatment, I felt that as chair of the governors, I should respond. It would have been wrong not to have challenged such outrageous comments to a group of governors who had sacrificed so much over many months to ensure the education, health and safety of over 200 young children.

Mark Durkan was in no hurry to leave and was most generous in the time he gave. He listened intently and was most helpful in what he explored with the governors. Some of the Stormont delegation indicated that they had to depart and I went with them to the monastery door to thank them for their visit and to wish them goodnight.

As Mr McNarry was leaving, I offered him a handshake and a 'goodnight'. He walked past me in silence and ignored my outstretched hand. This upset me. The next morning, I wrote to David Trimble pointing out that such behaviour was regrettable and did nothing to enhance the perception of his office as First Minister.

On 15 May, the First Minister wrote to me regretting 'anything during the meeting which caused me distress'. He further expressed his regret that the governors had been kept waiting at Parliament Buildings which meant that we had had to have a late-night meeting. This was appreciated. His explanation on the lack of a handshake by Mr. McNarry as he left the monastery was that 'Mr McNarry simply did not see the hand which you held out to him.' He also indicated that 'the darkness of the corridor' might have been a factor.

But darker days lay ahead. As already indicated, a great amount of time was spent looking at maps, plans, designs and correspondence coming from various agencies. All had one common denominator – namely, building a wall. No matter how often the school governors or the Ardoyne community pointed out that the *proposal* to build a wall and not its design was the issue, our words fell on deaf ears. It was always the concern of all to ensure that people everywhere in this area could feel secure in their own homes. Building a wall was one sure way of creating the opposite.

On 7 June, the First and Deputy First Minister wrote to me setting out the plans and time-scales on two main issues: community dialogue and community safety. Rightly, their letter pointed out 'that it is only through community dialogue that a lasting solution to tensions and divisions in the area can be found.' Their five-page letter had three appendices attached. The bottom line was that work on Ardoyne Road/Alliance Avenue was to begin at once.

The letter stated that at no stage had they been 'proposing to build a wall *across* [their emphasis] Ardoyne Road'. This was interesting but still a wall was to be constructed and presented all the problems already outlined. In a meeting on Sunday, 9 June, it had made clear that the proposed wall would be a danger to children going to and from school. The parents' views on how to move forward on the issues of safety and dialogue were sought, and it emerged that there was no desire to see these matters as being some kind of battle against the people of Glenbryn.

The day after the meeting, I wrote to David Trimble and Mark Durkan to let them know that meetings of school governors, parents and with teachers of Holy Cross Girls' School had rejected the building of a wall in any shape or form. The parents had reached a unanimous decision never to allow their children pass such a wall on their way to and from school.

The governors were not acting out of any desire to be disruptive but because of our responsibility to ensure the continued existence of Holy Cross School. In the letter, the position of the school governors was summed up as follows: 'Until such time as a wall has ceased to be part of your proposals the Board of Governors are not at liberty to enter into further discussions. To do so would be contrary to our obligation to keep the school operating.' The letter ended with a call for immediate face-to-face talks between all parties involved. On a personal level, I remained ready to enter into talks with the residents of Glenbryn on all issues affecting the situation.

On 7 June, the Concerned Residents of Upper Ardoyne released a statement on receipt of the letter from David Trimble and Mark Durkan. They expressed their shock at the contents of the letter, seeing it as a considerable backward step. Reading their statement, I could appreciate that all along they had been led to believe that a wall would be built. The only real issue was its design.

Now we had a serious situation arising in that both sides of the community, unionist and nationalist, were upset at what was being suggested. The people of Glenbryn concluded their statement by saying, 'we have been undermined and have no confidence that any further contact with them [the Ministers] will be productive.'

It was clear to me that David Trimble and Mark Durkan could not walk away from the construction of a wall as part of the resolution of the school protest. New designs, arbitration and so forth would follow, but the construction of the wall was to remain on their agenda. This was clearly stated in a letter on 14 June 2002 where the decision to erect a wall was made and it was merely its 'structure, features, materials and location' which remained at issue. It was at that stage in June 2002 that the school governors decided to seek a court injunction to prevent the work from proceeding. The legal document was lodged in the High Court of Justice, Queen's Bench Division, for leave to apply for judicial review of the decision of the First and Deputy First Ministers.

This was the easy part. Finding a way of doing this which would not destabilise the situation and put the children or the residents of Glenbryn in danger was far more difficult. There was also the matter of finding the finance for such a legal challenge. Application forms for legal aid were obtained and I began to complete them. The morning the judicial review application was to go into court, the Departmental Solicitor's Office proposed that the school governors would be given reasonable notice by the Office of the First and Deputy First Minister in advance of the commencement of works relating to the construction of a wall along Ardoyne Road. That morning, I was not in the court, but I received a telephone call from the school governors' solicitor asking if this was acceptable.

While there was no guarantee that the wall would not be built, there was the offer of a breathing space in which to resolve the issue. Also, this would spare Holy Cross Girls' School from being mentioned in court, with whatever publicity this might attract. Another factor was that it was difficult to see where we could find the money to finance the judicial review if the application for legal aid were not successful.

I agreed to this out-of-court resolution and was advised that, should the need arise in the future, it would be possible to revive the option of applying for judicial review. The summer came and went and, on 13 November 2002, I received a letter from Des Browne, MP, Parliamentary Under-Secretary of State. The previous month he had taken over a wider ministerial portfolio – and he reviewed the North Belfast situation as a whole.

In a detailed three-page letter, one sentence was of particular interest: 'Regarding the other element, that is to say the wall/fence proposal on Ardoyne Road, I am unable to proceed with it since it has not found sufficient consensus with both communities.' At long last, there was recognition that the agreement of November 2001 had never contained any reference to the building of a wall. It is still my opinion that the people in Glenbryn were misled by a verbal promise that they would get one.

Immediately on receipt of his letter, I wrote to the Minister, expressing relief that this conclusion had been reached, and indicating that the judicial review application would be withdrawn completely. On 23 November 2002, the *Irish News* reported that I had abandoned the High Court action now that the proposal to build the wall was gone.

Never at any stage was the court action seen by the school governors as being directed against the residents of Glenbryn. They had been led to believe at the suspension of the protest that the form of community safety promised would include some type of wall. It is quite understandable that they felt betrayed when this was not delivered.

The work of building trust between Glenbryn and Ardoyne was and still is a greater challenge. Looking back, it is better that no wall was built as it would have become the scene of more violence. While all is not perfect, there is an absence of violence on Ardoyne Road that gives an opportunity to search together for a deeper and more lasting peace than a wall could ever give. There are people on all sides of the divide who are genuinely concerned to create a better future in this small area of North Belfast. There are also people who don't want to see the past put behind us.

On 6 January 2003, Holy Cross Girls' School came under attack once again. That morning, the school opened as usual to welcome back the pupils after their Christmas break. The day was a Catholic holyday, and so Mass for the Feast of the Epiphany was to be celebrated in the school that morning. Shortly after the pupils were in school, a bomb was discovered at the school gate. The children were already in the Assembly Hall, and so we were caught in the dangerous position that if the school were evacuated and the bomb exploded, there would be terrible injuries and possibly loss of life. On the other hand, by keeping the children in school the accusation could be levelled at the school authorities that we had unnecessarily placed the lives of the children at risk.

It was decided to keep the children in the Assembly Hall while the Army bomb disposal unit worked on the device. Our hope had been that it would prove to have been a hoax. In fact, it was a live device and had the potential to maim and kill. In my own estimation, such a reckless act directed at defenceless children would not have had the support of the Glenbryn people. I made this known in subsequent interviews.

What was heartbreaking was that, once again, the memories of the past awful events were reawakened in the minds and hearts of these little ones. Their parents and families had to trust that all would be well as news of this latest attack spread through the community. There was some concern that the children had been kept in the school throughout the alert. I could not blame parents for such comments and tried to listen carefully to what they wanted should this arise again.

Just after 2 p.m. on Monday, 6 January 2003, the following message had been received by the BBC newsroom:

> The Red Hand Defenders claim responsibility for the pipe bomb at Holy Cross School this morning. The Board of Governors of the School have 7 days to close the school forever or else face action. RHD [a code word was given]

In such circumstances, the first thought of the governors was the impact any threatened action would have on the pupils. All the governors also had to assess the likely impact of any action not only on them but on their husbands/wives and children – (though this did not apply to the chair person of the governors!) The unanimous decision of the governors was to keep the school open and to refuse to bow to any form of intimidation. It was a great privilege for me to be associated with such courageous and generous people.

The following day, 7 January, a meeting was arranged between the Parent Teacher Association and the PSNI, in the school library. In most schools throughout the world, this would go unnoticed and be considered quite unworthy of comment. In Ardoyne, it was a sign of how important the safety of the children was to the parents and the school. In Ardoyne, relations with the police have never been easy or without problems.

That day the PSNI came to school out of uniform, and a most productive meeting was held. The parents made it clear, as did the school, that a police presence was essential every morning and afternoon. There were to be no exceptions to this practice and, in future, on the return to school after the holidays, the security forces were to check the school grounds for devices. This was to prove important in the future.

The police had scarcely dealt with the threat of 6 January when, on the afternoon of 8 January 2003, they visited me again at Holy Cross Monastery. This time they told me of a coded message from a male caller to the Samaritans. The caller claimed to be from an organisation named the Orange Volunteers, and stated that a list of named people would be dealt with for offences against the Upper Ardoyne residents. The inspector who delivered this message indicated that approximately ten names were on the list but he did not identify them. A walk around Ardoyne that afternoon after school quickly gave me the identities of quite a few people on that list. There were some who seemed surprised by their own inclusion on it.

This was yet another effort to destabilise the school. It was important that the children did not know of all that was happening. Some of those against whom threats were made had children at the school, and so there was a renewed sense of danger. The strength of the parents and the incredible support I felt personally made me so proud to be associated with this area and its people. But there was still more to come.

At first light on Monday, 1 September 2003, the army, with trained dogs, made a sweep of the grounds and the roads surrounding the school, and a bomb was discovered at the front gate. This time, there was no hesitation in making the decision that the school would not open until the all-clear was given. Once again, the bomb squad arrived and went to work on the cordoned-off Ardoyne Road.

It was heartbreaking to stand on Ardoyne Road at the police tape and tell parents that the school would not open at 9 a.m. as planned.

There were bright little faces of 4-year-olds who were beginning school for the first time. How to tell them that their school was under attack? It was arranged with the neighbouring St Gabriel's College that their gym could be used as a holding post until the emergency was over.

Teachers from Holy Cross Girls' School again showed their professional competence and their great warmth and love as they got the little children into groups as they arrived. Some of them had taken the brave step of risking sending their little one to Holy Cross, often against other family members' advice. Now they must have wondered if they had made the right decision.

It was mid-morning before Holy Cross School could open for its first day following the summer holidays. By this time, some parents had decided to take their children home and begin again the following day. They were wise as two further security alerts occurred in the area during the remainder of the morning.

Throughout everything, the governors have remained rock solid in their determination to keep the children safe and the school open. But to survive, the intake each year has to be sufficient to remain viable. Out of love for the school and in a desire to ensure its continuance, teachers have visited parents of school-going girls to ask them to consider supporting this parish school. The more I have seen and heard what they are prepared to do for education in this area, the more my admiration for these courageous and dedicated teachers. It would be so easy for any teacher to seek a position in some safer or less dangerous situation. But they didn't and they are the heroes.

As of May 2005, the enrolment is 172. You may recall that on the return to school in September 2001, the total was 225. Even allowing for a reduced school-going population this is a serious situation. It would be tragic if the school were to go out of existence because of the ongoing violence and the understandable reluctance of parents to see it as a safe place for their children. As recently as pre-Christmas 2004, I was called by the police during the night when a device was discovered lying at the front of the school. It was eventually dealt with before 3 a.m. and was found to be a hoax. But the underlying uncertainty continues.

Against this background, it is ironic that a hugely popular summer scheme for literacy and numeracy was not funded this year (2005) by the Belfast Education and Library Board. This is due in part to financial constraints, causing the number of schools taking part to be reduced. But the killer punch is that Holy Cross Girls' School does not qualify because its results are too good and so it does not fall within the criteria set out for participating schools. With the very turbulent history of their school, it is sad that the children had to be told this summer that there was 'no room at the inn'.

CHAPTER TWELVE

THE FIRST WEEK of January 2003 was eventful. There was the bomb to 'welcome' us back after Christmas, this was followed by two death threats within a matter of days of each other. When the end of the week arrived, I was happy to watch *The Late Late Show* on TV and get a good night's sleep.

On that Friday, 10 January 2003, as I got ready to go bed, I received a phone call from the police. It was from the same inspector who had visited me two days earlier with details of a death threat against me and others. As the call was to my mobile, he asked if I was in Holy Cross Monastery, and, when I replied that I was he asked me not to leave the monastery, as he wished to call to speak to me. It was not my intention to go anywhere but to bed.

Around midnight, the monastery doorbell rang. Letting the officer in, I noticed that there were at least two police land rovers outside the door. In the parlour, he handed me a sheet of paper. The message was as stark as it was brief: 'Intelligence indicates that Father Aidan Troy is to be killed before Monday.' The police station was Oldpark and the time on the document was 23.15 hours.

The officer whom I had known since my arrival in Ardoyne in 2001 began to explain to me what lay behind the simple words. He pointed out that this was not a phoned warning such as the two previous threats during the week had been. I asked what the difference was between a phoned warning and this one.

He explained that this was based on information that was in the possession of the police. He could not let me know how they had come by this information, but he stressed that it was totally reliable and that the threat was not an idle one. It meant exactly what it said. I was to be killed before Monday, 13 January 2003. It was as simple as that.

As he continued to talk about the seriousness of the situation, it became clear why there were several police jeeps outside the monastery. His strong advice to me was to leave immediately and go to somewhere safe. It was not his role to indicate where I should find safe haven but he indicated that if I were to cross into the Republic of Ireland for a while, it would make sense. To guarantee my safety, the police would escort me as far as the border.

While appreciating the advice, I knew at once that I was not leaving Holy Cross Monastery, that night or any other night, under threat. At length, the officer encouraged me to reconsider my decision. He again explained to me that the police intelligence was accurate and that I was about to be killed. He repeated that he could not go into detail but I got the distinct impression that he knew who was behind this threat on my life.

My reasoning was that if I left the monastery during the night, it would become known over the weekend that something had happened to cause me to leave without notice. In the light of the disruptive events of the previous week, it would become clear that something serious had taken me away. That weekend Fr Gary had an appointment outside Belfast and he was not due to return until the following evening.

The police officer wondered if I knew somewhere outside Belfast where I might be safer than remaining in Ardoyne, if I would not go out of Northern Ireland. One possibility was the Passionist Monastery in Crossgar, County Down, where I had lived when first ordained. This monastery is about 15 miles south of Belfast. Going there would not be an acceptable solution for me either, as it would still involve an unplanned departure from Holy Cross.

Looking back, I admire the patience of the officer as he tried, with some determination, to persuade me to get out of Ardoyne as quickly as possible. He was obviously in possession of more information than he could convey to me and it was a case of his trying to maintain confidentiality while letting me know that this threat was for real. I had no doubt that the threat was real but still it seemed unlikely to me that anything would happen. After more than an hour of conversation, he suggested that, over the coming weekend, I not use the car I usually drove. This indicated to me that he had some specific information that the attack on my life would come when I was in the car. That weekend, I had the usual calls to make that would involve using the car. There were hospitals to be visited and other such pastoral duties. Of course, I could use taxis but this would have indicated that something unusual had happened to cause me to discontinue using the car.

People in Ardoyne, after decades of violence, are razor sharp when it comes to noticing anything out of the usual. Had I gone away or changed the normal routine, I might as well have hung a notice on the front door, announcing that I was under a death threat. Despite what people might think of me, I hate letting attention focus on me personally. All that had happened to me since August 2001 had arisen from others and never from any desire on my part to be noticed or to become the focus of attention. That was why it was months later before knowledge of this threat became known.

Now that all appeals to leave Ardoyne and not to use the car had failed, the officer began to offer me advice for my own safety over the weekend. It was better if I varied my route as often and as randomly as possible. An example was that if I drove to the Mater Hospital on Crumlin Road, I should not return to Holy Cross by the same road. It was essential that I be particularly vigilant when stopped at traffic lights. When using the car, it was important that I walk around it and look for any signs of interference with it in even the smallest way. When turning on the ignition, it was important to leave the driver's door open. This would reduce the impact of any explosion and thereby lessen the severity of injuries.

All of this made sense and I appreciated the care and attention shown by the police. As the visit was ending, the officer suggested that I tell the other members of the Passionist community living in the monastery about the death threat. This was something I objected to as I knew it would cause me huge embarrassment. It was pointed out that they could possibly get caught up in some violence over the coming weekend. Reluctantly I agreed, but the telling was difficult and the reactions of my colleagues varied from a nod of the head to a smile. Above all times for it to happen Fr Gary was taken sick on his way back to Belfast. He phoned me to say that he was not well and was making for hospital in Belfast. He had not yet arrived in Newry and I advised him to go to outpatients at Daisy Hill Hospital. He was detained overnight, which meant that he was not around for the first two nights of that weekend.

More than an hour after his arrival, I saw the inspector out the front door of the monastery. He departed with the other police who had waited throughout our talk. It was past my bedtime. Much to my surprise, I fell asleep fairly quickly but I woke up earlier than usual. It was only then that it dawned on me that I might be in real danger. The night before, this had seemed just another threat. Now it dawned on me that there was someone or some group of people who had planned to kill me today or tomorrow.

Some of us as priests often encourage people to be trusting of God and his protection for his children. I had done so many times and, in recent years, had encouraged the parents to trust in God. They would be all right, I told them, and had nothing to fear, as God was close. Now it was different because it was my life that was under some very definite and specific death threat. I reverted to my traditional Catholic upbringing and made my way to Clonard Monastery where I asked for a Redemptorist priest to hear my confession. When he arrived, I asked if I could make a general confession. He was wonderful and, without the priest's knowing why I was making this confession, I left Clonard Monastery walking on air!

Truth be told, though, I was very vigilant at traffic lights and kept a close eye on cars and motorcycles alongside me. The doors of the car were kept locked and routes not usually used were taken on this bright Saturday morning. It was a strange feeling wondering if there was someone watching me and perhaps waiting for a suitable moment to kill me. It all seemed so unreal. However, the rest of that day passed without anything unusual happening. There was the usual round of duties in Holy Cross Church, such as Mass and confessions. It was unlikely that I was in any great danger in this setting but who could tell?

President and Dr McAleese came to hear of the death threat and phoned to express their concern. They assured me that I would be welcome as a guest but understood that I was not travelling south. An official of the Irish Government contacted me and offered me alternative accommodation in the Belfast area and the use of a car and driver. The outpouring of such concern was a humbling experience. There are so many wonderfully caring people in this world.

Saturday turned into Sunday and the usual round of pastoral activities. It was a bit strange greeting people after Mass and not being free to say a word about what was happening in my life. It made me realise how dangerous it is to judge other people. Who knows what is going on in the life of another person? There are many burdens carried that are not shared and, for that reason, weigh heavier.

By the time Sunday night came, I was growing tired of being careful. There are so many things a person does by rote without much thought. Now I had to think of what I was doing every time I left the monastery. It was also clear that routine was very much part of my life and it would not be difficult to predict where and when I might be found.

When I awoke on Monday morning, I realised that the threat had not materialised. I was still there to tell the tale. Of course, I did continue to look under the car and still took some precautions, but by Monday as I made my way to Holy Cross Girls' School, I had decided that the alert was most likely over and that life could return to what was regarded as normal.

It was a great relief that the weekend was over. Apart from my colleagues, nobody else was told by me about what had happened. When the story did eventually become public, I was deeply touched by the annoyance of so many of the parents who said that they would have wanted to know to offer support and help. There was a sense among them that we had shared so much over the months of the protest, and now I had not shared this threat with them.

Within a few days, other concerns took over and the memory of the death threats began to fade. Life had to go on, and, with it, the daily concern for a busy parish. There were the schools to be cared for and all the wonderful activities that go with them. There was also the Passionist community life and the need to address serious issues as vocations declined.

The year 2002 marked the Centenary of Holy Cross Church and, to celebrate it a pilgrimage to Rome was organised to take place the following year. Almost eighty of us pilgrims set off from Dublin in the footsteps of St Paul of the Cross, founder of the Passionists. As this was happening, a major restoration programme of Holy Cross Church was under way. All the planning and organising took up a great amount of time.

To create a transparent system of accounting for money raised to carry out this work, Holy Cross Ardoyne Trust was established. Many people gave of their time and professional expertise to support the efforts being made to create a better future for the people of this area, in the wake of the school protest. Fundraising trips to America were organised. Groups like the AOH and the Ladies Ancient Order of Hibernians could not have done more to support the 'refounding' of Holy Cross. I can recall speaking at grand banquets throughout the United States and in tiny bars. There were just so many people who wanted to be part of a new start for Ardoyne. It was humbling to stand in these places and listen to people express their admiration for the pupils, parents and school staff of Holy Cross.

Visiting New York for St Patrick's Day, I met up with Mick McCarthy, former Republic of Ireland soccer manager, who was there with his wife, Fiona. He was aware of the happenings at Holy Cross and was one of the first to make a personal donation. There were so many good and helpful people who wanted to help.

The memories of the death threats may have ceased to have any significant place in my life or activity but the police had not forgotten. In early February 2003, the same police inspector who had told me of the death threats asked me to consider applying to the Northern Ireland Office for inclusion in 'Key Person Protection Scheme'. The Secretary of State for Northern Ireland operates a limited, non-statutory, discretionary scheme under which physical protection measures can be provided, at public expense, at the homes of people who are assessed by the Chief Constable to be at significant or serious threat. The purpose of the scheme is to protect those individuals whose death or injury as a result of terrorist attack could damage or seriously undermine the democratic framework of government.

It is obvious that this scheme cannot protect all people who may be under some degree of threat. A judgement has to be made by the Secretary of State about who will be included. The onus of responsibility is on the applicant to present their case as fully as possible to the Northern Ireland Office. Basic to all applications for consideration were details of present occupation and details of any personal threats or attacks suffered. When I asked what practical difference becoming part of this scheme would make in my case, I was given a list advising that my bedroom door would be reinforced, protective clothing suggested and other such measures taken. I was totally bewildered by the suggestion that I should consider applying for inclusion in this protection scheme.

From the evening of my arrival in Belfast at the end of July 2001 to February 2003, I could not believe that anybody would want to kill me. It was and remains my conviction that I had done nothing of any significance in Ardoyne since my arrival that could merit such an extreme measure as becoming part of a key person protection programme. Without a trace of mock humility, I knew and still know that I was not and am not a key person. What I did was what anybody with an ounce of humanity in them would do when they see children being abused.

With as much humour and courtesy as I could, I told the police officer that I had no intention of applying for such a scheme. He was used to my style and, rather than spend hours trying to persuade me as he had on the night of 10 January, he left without much debate.

However, he came back to visit me soon again. If I would not apply for inclusion in this scheme, would I object if the police applied for special protection? Not wishing to appear ungrateful, and also with a certain amount of curiosity, I agreed. It made me wonder why the police had made this suggestion. Did they have knowledge of some continuing threat on my life? If they did, I certainly did not receive any new information from them.

It was still hard for me to take this matter all that seriously. On 2 March, I got around to compiling the information needed to support the police application on my behalf. Apart from personal details, I had to give an account of locations regularly visited, any personal listings, car details, any role that might attract attention, public profile, media references and threats or attacks.

It was just as well that I was not worried about my safety as I heard nothing over the coming weeks. On 20 May, I wrote to the Northern Ireland Office requesting some information about the police application on my behalf. My concern was made urgent in that an intruder had gained entry to the monastery at 3 a.m. some weeks previously. Fortunately, robbery was his motive and no personal harm was done to any member of the community living in the monastery.

The following day, 21 May, Security Minster Jane Kennedy, wrote a detailed letter regarding the application made on my behalf by the local police in North Belfast. Her first consideration in deciding if an individual should be admitted to the scheme related to the applicant's occupation. Her next consideration was whether the applicant has any wider public role. Thirdly, the provision of physical home security measures is dependent upon advice from the Chief Constable that the person concerned is under a serious or significant threat of terrorist attack.

The Security Minister's next sentence brought her decision: 'Regarding your case, I have now received advice from the Chief Constable indicating that you are not considered by him to be under a serious or significant threat.' She concluded that protection of the monastery was not warranted at that time.

This would have been my own assessment of my security situation, but it did strike me as strange in some ways that the North Belfast police making the application were turned down because of the assessment of their own Chief Constable.

Jane Kennedy suggested that, if I wished, I could speak to the local PSNI District Commander or seek advice and assistance from the Crime Prevention Officer. Like many other people, I was given a copy of the red booklet 'Personal Protective Measures'.

There have been occasional incidents where I have been threatened. In April 2005, I was accosted by a group of loyalists in the Mater Hospital, Belfast, when I was visiting parishioners. This group was waiting for the lift to arrive when I walked past. Some less than complimentary remarks were made after I had walked past. I went back and asked the men and women if they would like to say to my face what had just been said behind my back. They did repeat the same remarks, and, as they waited for the lift to arrive, I had the opportunity to engage with them verbally. We did not reach total agreement but I felt that it was better to engage face to face than to let cat-calls behind my back go unchallenged.

Fortunately, such incidents are few and far between. The number of people who have spoken to me in a positive way far exceeds the number of such negative incidents. It still amazes and embarrasses me when people speak or write to me offering some praise or complimentary remarks, but it is not possible to accept the latter without living with the few negative or threatening comments.

Overall, people are generous in their comments and encouragement. It has been a great source of strength to hear from people all over the world who let me know that they are praying for us at Holy Cross. When the suicides in North Belfast became known, a similar outpouring of prayer and support arrived at the monastery. In 2005, there are still generous people who are volunteering to help young people at risk and to offer support for families bereaved by suicide.

In November 2004, I had decided to take up the offer of my Provincial Superior in Dublin that I take a break. He suggested this in light of the events just described here and because a long-term programme of renewal of Holy Cross lay ahead. In a most positive conversation, one option among others that he put to me was to take a break of at least a few months. While the situation in North Belfast was not perfect, it was no longer necessary to make the twice daily visits to Holy Cross Girls' School. The work on restoring Holy Cross Church was reaching an advanced stage, and plans were taking shape to vacate Holy Cross Monastery and build a smaller residence for a few

Passionist members. As will be seen in the next chapter, plans for the reopening of the derelict Family Centre had taken an interesting turn.

In 2003, I had bumped into a representative of Currach Press who had asked me was I going to write a book about Holy Cross and all that had happened since I had arrived there. This amused me as I had never seriously considered that I could write a book about these extraordinary events.

In my own estimation, I had not played a significant role. The key 'players' were the children, the parents, the teachers and staff of the school, the school governors, the other schools of the parish and area, other individuals and the wider community of Ardoyne, the residents of Glenbryn and others who travelled to the daily protest, the police, the military and the media.

I could understand a journalist such as Anne Cadwallader writing the book, *Holy Cross: The Untold Story*, because she had reported the events on an almost daily basis. But it had not crossed my mind to do the same. People presumed that I had kept diaries and copies of correspondence from the period, but I had never seen the events between my arrival in late July and the suspension of the protest on 23 November 2001 as some sort of 'event' or 'campaign' that I should record. The happenings were nothing more and nothing less than children going to and from school, and my role, as I saw it from beginning to end, was to be supportive of the parents as the primary educators of the children. Moreover, I learned quickly that, as chair of the school governors, I was obliged to care along with others for the health and safety of the children and to see that a high-quality education was delivered. I did both of these to the best of my ability. It was only when the parents asked me to walk with them that I did so. After I had walked once, I could not stop until I knew that both they and their children were safe.

Around the world I have been humbled by peace and reconciliation awards that have been conferred on me. While grateful for the recognition of the parish in which I am asked to serve, I am also profoundly embarrassed. The real heroes are the children for their incredibly forgiving and loving attitude over a long period of hatred directed at them. Next to them, I will never forget the dignity and restraint of the parents and guardians of these children as they saw their flesh and blood targeted. The popular perception of Ardoyne since 1969 and long before is of a place where tough people live and people who can act in a violent way. It was heartbreaking for me to see grown men cry tears of frustration when they were not able to defend their little girls. I saw mothers decline into pale shadows of their former selves, because of the pain of watching their little ones being abused. It broke my heart to hear of how brothers and sisters of these pupils, both older and younger, were worried sick because of the twice daily risk of going to and from school.

Anybody who claims that these were not the ones to be saluted and honoured has failed to understand what the Holy Cross School protest was about. Some people might have perceived that I was on a personal ego trip but nothing could be further from the truth. I have come to the world of media and public image far too late in life. I am intensely shy by nature and still find it difficult when people recognise me and speak to me. Some people enjoy being recognised, but I'm not and never was one of them.

In deciding to accept the offer of the Provincial Superior to take a break from Holy Cross, there was also the factor of my health. God has gifted me with a robust constitution, and the local doctor and nurse were most caring in dealing with any minor ailments that arose. After much thought and some advice I asked the members of the Holy Cross Passionist Community on 7 December 2004 if they were in agreement with my going away in January 2005 for a break. It was a humbling experience for me to hear the three members present indicate their full and unqualified support for my request.

Christmas 2004 was one in which I really felt totally at peace. The message of peace and happiness filled my heart. With thanks to God for such a great opportunity to find rest and listen in prayer to what God was saying to me, I planned to leave Ardoyne shortly after the dawn of the New Year. However, an unexpected event happened that delayed me. A young child of 21 months was discovered dead in the early days of January 2005. All children, as I had discovered, are special, and baby Michael was very special to his parents and his sisters and brother. Having sat through the nights of the wake with the family and the neighbours, I left Ardoyne on Monday, 10 January 2005.

For almost two decades, I had the privilege of conducting school and community retreats for the Religious of Christian Education in Ireland and England. Our Lady's School, Rathnew, County Wicklow was a boarding school in which I had conducted school retreats year after year. Attached to the school property is a gate lodge and this was put at my disposal for the break I was taking. This was a wonderful rural setting.

The early days of my break in Rathnew were not easy in that I felt guilty about being away and leaving a heavier burden on the three active priests back at Holy Cross. As the days turned into weeks, I relaxed more and realised that when I got back, one of the others could go away for a prolonged break. As vocations to the priesthood and religious life decline, I believe that it is important that we take care of each other in active ministry. By going away myself, I hoped to give something of a lead to my colleagues to do the same.

Before leaving Holy Cross, I had issued an open invitation to any of the priests who wished to visit me while in Rathnew, but nobody took up the offer. However, it was not possible to be completely away as I had some engagements I felt it wrong to break. It was possible for me to attend a Board of Management meeting of St. Brendan's College, Bray, of which I am a member. It was an honour to preach during Church Unity Octave at the Bray Churches Together liturgy. And one afternoon, I went back to Belfast to address a group of Presbyterian ministers who had invited me to speak to them.

In early February, I was pleased to be able to fulfil an invitation to speak at a debate. It was good to renew acquaintance with David Irvine, MLA, and Mary Lou McDonald, MEP, and to meet Jim Allister, MEP, and Senator Martin Mansergh. The huge gathering of students that night was wonderful to address and I enjoyed listening to their comments and observations.

On Ash Wednesday, 9 February 2005, I was pleased to celebrate Mass for the staff and pupils of Clermont School, Rathnew, on whose property I was living. The next day, the Leaving Certificate pupils welcomed me for a question and answer session. Their energy and the scope of their questions were truly impressive. On the educational front, I came back twice to Belfast for teacher interviews and in mid-February, I went to Larne to direct a vocations retreat of prospective candidates for the Diocese of Down and Connor. The Mass on the second day was celebrated by Bishop Walsh and I joined him in the sanctuary. After the Mass, we chatted about my time away and he expressed the hope that I would be back to Holy Cross at the end of it.

During my period of leave, I was also able to attend the court hearing in Dublin of the appeal of Dermot Laide for his conviction for manslaughter outside Anabel's nightclub in south Dublin. It was good being able to meet him each day and spend some time with his parents and family. It is my belief that this whole case needs to be reviewed.

Each day, I tried to discipline myself to write. There were also wonderful opportunities to get out in the fresh air to walk or jog. One day I went to Leopardstown Races, and of course there were family and friends to catch up with during this most special time. To put it simply, this was a wonderful time in my life. With the help of an experienced spiritual director I was able to reflect on where the Spirit was leading me. My regret was that I had not done this before but I was so grateful to God and my brethren in Holy Cross for this time of growth and grace.

Each year, the Provincial Superior makes an official visit to each Passionist community. The visit to Ardoyne was scheduled for 25 and 26 February. I was told by him that it would be sufficient for me to have my talk with him in his office in Dublin rather than returning to Belfast. It was great being able to tell him how well I felt, how much I had benefited from this break, and how anxious I was that one of the other three in the community would plan to go away when I got back. From Dublin, I went back to my cottage with a song in my heart and a prayer that the Provincial Superior's visit to Ardoyne would go well.

Shortly after this meeting with the Provincial, I was invited to visit the White House for St. Patrick's Day. The American Consul in Belfast, Mr Dean Pittman, was keen that I be one of a small group of people who would meet President George W. Bush before he addressed the general group. He would be accompanied by An Taoiseach, Bertie Ahern, and Mitchell Reiss, American Envoy to

Northern Ireland. Feeling that this might make a good conclusion to my break I accepted the invitation.

The visit to Washington was truly memorable. There was some criticism that I had met President Bush following his declaration of war on Iraq. It is possible for me to see why such an argument would be made. However, as this book tries to show, ruling certain people in and others out does not lead to healing and reconciliation.

The call of the Gospel and the religious life that I entered over forty years ago calls for risk-taking in the name of creating a better life and advancing the Kingdom that Christ came to establish on earth. Many years ago, I took a course at university, entitled 'The Anatomy of Human Greatness'. The lives of people like Gandhi, Martin Luther King and Dorothy Day, were studied to try to establish why they had made such a difference. The results of this study were fascinating. Among other findings was that these people took the circumstances around them as they found them and tried to find where there were points of growth. This often meant taking risks to the extent that, if they got it wrong, not only might their project or dream not happen, but they might not survive themselves. It was as radical as that.

I could never aspire to be numbered in such a list of great people. But I do believe that everyone can take their own immediate circumstances and see how changes in the mosaic before them can change despair to hope and death to life. It is the working out of the Gospel contradiction that the first shall be last and the last first. We have to be ready to be patient and know that the changes that matter will come from within and not from some new and spectacular outside intervention.

The tragedy is that, as the Church and communities of religious women and men in the western world find that the number of candidates has decreased, we have begun in some places to circle the wagons and to look inwards. This can lead to sick communities, and their death certificate is guaranteed unless some new light is allowed shine into the dark places. It is true that the darkness can seem greatest just before the dawn.

As the events of the Holy Cross School protest enter into the history of the brave people of Ardoyne, it is clear that our Passionist community is called to make radical decisions. We now number four members living at Holy Cross and three others in nursing care. It was clear to me soon after I arrived, that all was not well in the arrangements at Holy Cross. In setting out my hopes and dreams three days after I arrived I highlighted some issues that had been known for years which would require attention.

Reading that document again, I can see that I got some aspects right and some wrong. There is no doubting that openness and dialogue continued to develop as I suggested but they did not have the transparency that would have made such a difference.

On the other hand, the suggestion I made to establish a 'media desk' to comment on church life and life in wider society developed in a way that I could not have foreseen. Each member of the community has featured in media in some shape or form over the past four years. The criticisms often made of media have valid points but the potential of proper use of the media for evangelisation and the development of people is immense. The late Pope John Paul II is a shining example of one who brought Christ to many through a wise use of modern media.

The core of the community life at Holy Cross I set out in those early days as prayer, both individual and community celebrations. Personal prayer must be a private matter in many ways. Because of personal choices and parish and ministry pressures, we never quite got the communal prayer and liturgical celebrations to the point I would have wished.

As the one who was last to arrive, I could see how difficult was the task that I was facing. Some members of the community have been in Holy Cross for over fifty years and others for a long number of years. The Provincial may have designated me as 'superior' by title, but being 'junior' might be a more accurate job-description. To effect change was always going to be difficult.

And so it has proved to be. As one lady put it when disagreeing with something I had said, 'You may be only here for a short while and just passing through'. The weight of tradition can be enriching in some ways, but it can also be a heavy burden on the newcomer.

Most of my involvement at Holy Cross is with the people of the area and much further afield. The hectic rate of activity and the intensity of involvement lie at the heart of my sense of blessing in being at Holy Cross. With hand on heart, I can say that it would be difficult to find a people more wonderful to serve.

I came to Holy Cross as a result of obedience and found that in all my years as a Passionist and priest, this has been the most blessed part of my life. I am free to stay and serve and would love to end my days in Ardoyne. Equally, I have to face the possibility that I may be asked to leave. I cannot but think of the attitude of Job:

Naked I came from my mother's womb,
naked I shall return.
The Lord gave, the Lord has taken back.
Blessed be the name of the Lord!
If we take happiness from God's hand
must we not take sorrow too?

CHAPTER THIRTEEN

SOME OF THE best lessons I have learned in life have come from the mistakes I have made. When all is working out well, it is possible to think that it will always be so. What are the lessons to be learned from the Holy Cross School protest?

The fact that school-children were targeted needs some examination. There are still people who will deny this and say that the adult population was actually the target of the protest. The other important fact is that it was a Catholic school that was blockaded. If Holy Cross Girls' School had existed in some sort of isolated cocoon from neighbouring schools, it might have been said that an unknown school, its pupils and teachers came under attack. But in fairness to all the schools of North Belfast sincere efforts were ongoing to bridge the divide.

Holy Cross Girls' School had excellent programmes of co-operation with Wheatfield School, the neighbouring state school directly across the road from it. Yet when the protest began, that past co-operation did not play an effective role in stopping it. It was regrettable that some former friends now ended up on opposite sides of this bitter dispute. The same breakdown occurred, as we have seen, between some of the churches of the area and their clergy. My role in any failure in this matter is deeply regretted and I publicly ask forgiveness. The regular meetings now taking place on a monthly basis are based on scripture and friendship. We have moved a long way from polite conversation over tea and biscuits. It will take time to find the confidence to address issues together.

Unless clergy of different denominations in this area can speak with one voice, the Gospel will judge us as having failed. There are some people from all church congregations who are appalled at our efforts to establish the Kingdom in our streets and among people of all outlooks. There are still people who criticise the priest for having time to be on the streets when trouble erupts. A recent anonymous letter with a Dublin postmark asked me to go back to the monastery and say my prayers rather than being present on the streets.

There is a crying need for church leaders, bishops and moderators, to address the issues of North Belfast in the wake of the bitterness left behind after the Holy Cross School protest. If they are slow to do so, we could invite more trouble down the road. There are so many people who are looking for leadership. Young people are as generous as ever but find many of us lacking in inspiration.

There are people who would never protest on Ardoyne Road because it is not the respectable thing to do but who harbour bitterness and have an unforgiving heart. As recently as May 2005, some good church-going Protestant people made it clear to their clergy that I would not be welcome at a cross-community meeting to search for peace and reconciliation. The reason they gave was that my role during the Holy Cross School protest was still a matter of hurt to them. It is interesting that people in the Protestant community who have less attachment to church services are more ready to engage with me and other Catholics across religious and political lines.

Scratch the surface and sectarianism in some shape or form emerges. None of us is free from this scourge within the society that is Northern Ireland. Much has been written and spoken on this topic. Some progress is being made by people of good-will to resolve the divisive issues that keep us apart. Church unity in Ardoyne is not an academic issue but an urgent requirement.

Unity of Christians requires theological leadership at the highest level of the churches. However, there is also the need to address the issue of church unity at ground level. There will be no remedying of the deep divisions that are part and parcel of life in most areas of

Northern Ireland until we drop our caution and tackle our fears.

No matter how theologically well-intended, a document like the declaration *Dominus Jesus* in 2000 from the late Pope John Paul II caused some distress to Protestant churches. The declaration contains some wonderful aspirations to achieving the unity for which Christ prayed among all his people. But that fine document will be best remembered for paragraph 17 where we read, 'the ecclesial communities which have not preserved the valid Episcopate and the genuine and integral substance of the Eucharistic mystery are not Churches in the proper sense.'

This deserves a bigger debate than can be entered into here. However, if a draft of any such document had first been seen in any divided community like Belfast or elsewhere, hurt might have been avoided. Often the first we know of a document from local bishops or from the Vatican is when it arrives and we are asked to accept it. How much dialogue is there in such a way of acting? It seems to me that the Holy Spirit is also present among the people of God as well as in the hierarchy and in the papacy.

Football may seem a long way from a scholarly declaration like *Dominus Jesus*, but even in 2005 there may be more connections than seem likely at first sight. Rangers play Celtic in Scottish soccer and rioting can follow. Following the end of the Scottish soccer season in 2005, rioting broke out, resulting in injury to both rioters and police. One lady watching the tragedy unfold said more to herself than to anyone around here, 'The bitterness will never be mended.' She said it more in sorrow than in anger.

Another example better known to people born in Northern Ireland than to me is the 'marching season' from Easter until the end of August with all that goes with it. There are places where bus stops are segregated along religious lines reminiscent of the worst days of the apartheid system in South Africa. Of course, nobody designates these bus stops for one group or another but de facto that is how we have adapted to living in a deeply divided and suspicious society.

The marching season of 2005 proved a difficult one in Ardoyne. Out of 3,000 marches most pass through non-contentious neighbourhoods. A few are different. Derry has developed an impressive means to dialogue on contentious marches. Yet even there in July 2005 there was an outbreak of disturbances.

In Ardoyne, sincere and intensive efforts were made to create opportunities for young people to have an alternative to waiting for something to happen as marches passed. Football, boxing, music and dancing were all organised and well supported. On 12 July through the generosity of President and Dr McAleese 100 children from Ardoyne were guests in Áras and Uachtaráin in Dublin. Peaceful morning and evening protests against sectarian marches past people's homes passed over without incident. Dialogue with police and military helped to eliminate any surprises. It all seemed so good until the very end of the day when serious rioting broke out. Truthfully, the first missiles were thrown from the nationalist side. Water cannon followed later by rubber bullets did nothing to calm the situation. The night ended on a sinister note when dissident republicans threw blast bombs over the police screens on Crumlin Road. A journalist was carried away injured. Over 100 police suffered varying degrees of injury. It was heartbreaking after such great efforts to avoid this to know that once again Ardoyne would make the headlines for all the wrong reasons.

One news bulletin drew parallels with the Holy Cross Schools dispute. The blessing is that by the time the marching season is in full swing, the schools are closed for summer holidays. Otherwise, I would dread to think of what might happen.

Neither the Parades Commission that determines the routes of parades nor the police can sort this contentious issue without a basic dialogue happening between the Loyal Orders and the local residents. The Orange Order is opposed to such engagement. If it persists in this stance, there is a real danger that not only will violence continue, but it will be a miracle if a life is not lost. People intent on unravelling the peace process will use occasions such as loyalist marches to create havoc. The local people and politicians have no interest in allowing violence to return to the streets of Ardoyne or anywhere else.

If I have learned one lesson from Holy Cross, it is that divisions are so deep that it is reasonable to conclude that they will not be easily healed. But suppose we were to think the unthinkable and question where we should go in the design of education for a better future? The seeds of sectarianism need to be tackled from crèche onwards through the whole education system.

Let me be clear in stating that I am not suggesting that the present system of education is responsible for sectarianism. However, because housing is so arranged along religious and political lines, people often don't meet people of another religion until they begin studying at third level colleges, and not every young person keeps in education that long. What if for a moment we were to dream and imagine a crèche opening its door to all who would arrive? There would be no possibility of this happening at present, but what about in the long term?

Since the creation of this political entity, we have not succeeded in eliminating hatred and separation. Of course, education alone cannot hope to carry the weight of reconciliation and peace in this divided island. But just because it cannot eliminate the horror of recurring violence since the 1920s does not mean that it does not have a pivotal role to play in this millennium in seeing an end to the hatred, bigotry and killing. The alternative is to adopt the line of the woman at the Celtic/Rangers riot, 'The bitterness will never be mended.'

Early on in this book I pointed out that I know very little about the philosophy and practice of education in this part of Ireland. Four years on, that is still true. However, I have seen enough to convince me that something new and radical needs to be attempted. If we don't go back to the roots of separation and division, we are condemned to go on repeating our past mistakes.

At present, we have three main school groups. Catholic schools are a key part of the Catholic Church's mission and have a long and honourable history. Great sacrifices have been made by generations of parents, teachers, priests and bishops, benefactors and children themselves to make us rightly proud of now having a superbly educated Catholic population. This has had a great effect in ensuring good employment and a standard of living way beyond what was possible in the last century.

In the Catholic Church, education pays regard to the formation of the whole person. Moreover, education is seen not only as a means for the promotion of a better society but also as a platform to lead the student eventually to eternal life. This holistic approach aims to address the physical, moral and intellectual gifts of the student, so that there is a harmonious development. This development leads to a sense of responsibility and a right use of freedom, enabling the person to play an active part in social life. In essence, this is what the Church's Code of Canon Law has to say on education.

It is my experience that Catholic schools rightly insist on an ethos that is conducive to the distinctive philosophy and values of Catholic education. Most Rev. Seán Brady, Archbishop of Armagh, sees Catholic schools as best defined by their values: love, solidarity, truth, justice and the pursuit of the common good. It has been my happy experience to have seen teachers in Catholic schools who not only teach these values, but who embody them in their own lives.

All writing on Catholic education will acknowledge that the context in which it takes place is fundamental. The theological exploration of the 'Inculturation' of the Gospel has helped us to see that the eternal values of Jesus are never in a 'one fits all' model. There is uniqueness in the context in which Jesus comes to establish his Kingdom. Our context is one that is characterised by profound conflict, and this leads to an urgent need to break down barriers of ignorance, misunderstanding and suspicion.

While schools cannot bear the full responsibility of creating a just and respectful society in which reconciliation is practised, it is my belief that they are part of the solution. Unfortunately, however, there is defensiveness in the Catholic Church when an examination of Catholic schools is mentioned, and words such as disloyalty or lack of fidelity to the Church come to the surface.

In 1998, the Good Friday (Belfast) Agreement stated that 'an essential aspect of the reconciliation process is the promotion of a culture of tolerance at every level of society.' In November 2001, as the Holy Cross protest was nearing suspension, the Catholic bishops of Northern Ireland issued a document, 'Building Peace Shaping the Future'. In this comprehensive document on education, one of a long series of excellent documents, the bishops envisage Catholic schools 'as being ideally placed to assist our society to move beyond its deeply ingrained divisions into a new coherence and openness to the world at large'. They point out the basis for this assertion as 'our theology of reconciliation and [...] our promotion of the common good'.

There is no doubting the sincerity of these words and had I not walked up and down Ardoyne Road for almost three months, I would not have even thought of questioning them. But now, in truth, I must.

The reason for my doing so leads me to the second group of schools operating in Northern Ireland. These are state schools which, by and large, are attended by Protestant children. This is particularly true at primary level. For reasons of clarity, it is generally true to regard these schools as having a Protestant ethos and outlook. This is not a judgement of value but rather a statement of fact.

Ardoyne Road is a good example of a place where children from 4 to 11 years of age are educated in primary schools that directly face each other. As already pointed out, these two schools have co-operated in a truly impressive fashion over the years. But they will always be two schools and never reach deep enough to bridge the gap of inherited division, suspicion and sad to say, mutual fear. The dedication of the two school staffs did much to improve mutual understanding and development, but once the 19 June hostilities broke out, these were smashed in one afternoon.

In that situation, we retreat back to our own side, and the way back to love and trust is heartbreaking in its slowness and fragility. Suppose in a moment of madness we had those two schools on the one campus and the Catholic, Protestant, Muslim and whoever were together from this tender age. Suppose further, that they already knew each other from crèche and play school. Imagine if the parents stood at the same school gate to collect their little ones.

This is cutting through a huge swathe of history and theology. But if our building of peace is to shape the future, something like this needs to be attempted. It will not be easy to achieve this new way of educating the children for a new future and it is tempting to say that the mechanics of creating this new approach are complicated. This is true but the dream of giving the children life to the full is more fundamental. Imagine if we allowed children do what they do best – play, make friends, argue, laugh and cry. Suppose that it was only later that they were gently led to learn that the adult world suffers from the sickness of sectarianism and hatred.

And suppose they were later to learn that their church is committed to working towards unity with others churches to which their friends belong. To move forward on church unity will remove the causes of so much hurt and so many tears such as we saw on Ardoyne Road in 2001.

It is comparatively easy to look at the question of church unity in Rome. I know I did it during university studies in 2000-2001, and within weeks of writing what passed for educated papers on this topic of unity, I saw the raw results of church disunity. I would have loved to have brought some of the professors and heads of Vatican departments to see what the sin of disunity can bring to little children. If the Kingdom belongs to such as these, as Jesus suggests, we adults have a lot to answer for by our holding out on finer points of theology.

It would be my impression that many of the protestors and Holy Cross parents had not such points of theology in mind as they watched division unfold and children scream in terror. Yet in the name of fidelity to their particular church, children are labelled by the separate school system.

After primary school, many of Northern Ireland's children will go on to their own denominational school. Of course, Catholic schools are not just for Catholics but are open to all who wish to attend. I have given school retreats in England where, in a convent school, Catholics were in the minority. Jews, Anglicans and the non-baptised formed the majority and had not one moment's hesitation in entering into all that was offered in the annual retreat. Many of these children had grown up together and while they knew that they were of different religions they also knew that humanity was the first bond between them. They started with Genesis and the creation of each person in the image and likeness of God.

The other main group in the education system is Integrated Education. Integrated schools are to be found at both primary and secondary levels. There is a great growth in this sector and many parents look to them as the best option to break out of the circle of sectarianism and division. Talking to these parents, I have been greatly impressed by their willingness to take the risk of trying something that is not always supported by their clergy or relatives. It is not always as easy as people outside of Ireland might imagine, and it is not unknown for children from the same integrated school to end up on different sides of the same riot in their home locality. This is tragic but gives us reason to be cautious in seeing such schools as the best solution to educational needs.

It is my belief that these integrated schools are asked to carry a heavy burden. In many ways they are asked to unite a deeply divided society. With so much housing being segregated, it is asking a lot of the school to attempt to integrate people living separate lives. Their achievements are to be lauded and appreciated.

It is clear that powerful benefactors like the US Government see this as the way forward and are generous in their financial support. On St Patrick's Day 2005 President George W. Bush warmly welcomed two delightful pupils from an integrated school in Northern Ireland. My hope and prayer is that the Catholic bishops, the Government and the integrated sector will open up a dialogue to seek to create a new way of educating children for a better future. It would be wrong of me even to suggest what the outcome of these talks could be, but not to explore together is to guarantee that the limitations of the present structure will go on to present us with issues that simply will not go away.

Maybe what is suggested here will not give us anything better than we have at present. But to know this will leave us richer in our dedication to education and a better future for all children. It is essential that we start from the child and the child's needs. To start with systems and administration is to lose the Gospel window that sees the child as the embodiment of the Kingdom. Do we have the right to settle for what we have at present, no matter how good it is? The call is to trust God and each other enough to cast out into the deep and know that we will be safe because that is often where Christ is found.

To back up the dream of a better future as part of the legacy of the Holy Cross protest, I was amazed one day to see that right outside the front door of Holy Cross Monastery there is a real possibility to take a step towards reconciliation and peace. The original Holy Cross

Schools, Boys' and Girls', are now a derelict wreck. Once upon a time, they thrived as schools and many a senior resident of Ardoyne has told me of the lessons given and all the other experiences that make up school. School days are often better in their retelling than when we go through them! As numbers grew in the parish, bigger buildings were needed and so school buildings sprang up in other areas of the parish.

The now unused school buildings were adapted and became an important Family Centre. A crèche, classes in cookery, sewing and many other great activities took place within the walls of this building. The intensity of the Troubles made this building a dangerous place much of the time. Attacks were frequent and fire did an amount of damage. With great regret, it was decided that the Family Centre would have to close its doors, and people were left without a place they loved and appreciated.

Serious efforts were made during the 1990s to find a formula that would enable the Family Centre to reopen. By the time I arrived in summer 2001, these good efforts had not yet reached fruition. Maybe God has other plans for this strategically placed building straddling the dividing line between Ardoyne and Woodvale. Following the deep divisions revealed and exacerbated during the protest of 2001, it came to me that the Family Centre could rise from the ashes to be the lasting legacy of the Holy Cross School protest. The building is wonderfully placed with one door opening onto the Woodvale Road (Protestant) and the door on the other side of the building opening onto Holy Cross parish. There was a time in our history when people could come in one door and leave by another. That freedom to come and go must be our aim. There can be no future in a life that sees us for all time living apart and suspicious of any move towards each other. The dream is that sooner rather than later, the doors of a refurbished Family Centre will open to all who have the love of children and of their future in their hearts.

Why not open a cross community crèche and let the children find from day one that children are born equal and of eternal value? It is adults who declare the differences.

Why not open an internet café in the Family Centre and let our young people know that the World Wide Web has more to unite us than anything that divides us in North Belfast?

Why not encourage our weightlifters and boxers to train and compete together as athletes?

Why not ask our statutory bodies to provide an information office that would address housing needs, health requirements and all those other services that we all need?

Why not be creative and let all sorts of good and valuable activities and skills be open to all on the basis of wish and need? The entry will not be determined by politics or religion but by a desire to share this part of God's creation.

People have told me that this will never happen and, after events in summer 2005, I can appreciate what they are saying. Those more experienced than me tell me that, had I been born in Ardoyne, I wouldn't be so naïve as even to suggest such a venture. I am enormously respectful of those who have suffered more than I have. So many families are still grieving for a loved one and find it next to impossible to see how doors can ever be opened.

These people may be right and I will be the first to admit this if I am proved wrong. In the meantime, however, there are some wonderful people who have read what I have written and shared this dream.

People from different parts of the island of Ireland have come to me and offered to become part of this new way of being neighbours. Through constant and patient work, the most unlikely people have begun to examine what is being proposed for this Family Centre. It is still hard to believe how far the project has advanced. Parishioners have been the backbone of the restoration of all aspects of Holy Cross including the Family Centre. Through intermediaries, I have sat at table with some of the 'Brigadiers' from loyalist paramilitaries and had a meal during which we looked together at what can only be described as a 'map of peace'. On the republican side I have met some leading members and asked what their views were on the map of peace. They too have been generous and courteous in their assessment.

Professional people have been courageous also in becoming involved in what is a highly unusual project. Without their expert advice, our discussions would be nothing but vague aspirations. Their participation is another sign of hope for this dream seeing the light of day some time in the near future.

None of this work can succeed without financial support, and there is a most wonderful outpouring of support and encouragement from events as diverse as a little girl doing a sponsored skip, and a Gala Ball at the Europa Hotel, in Belfast, to golf outings, a draw for cars and the daily goodness of people who give not of what is superfluous but out of their need. Organisations like Lions' Clubs and Ancient Order of Hibernians have rallied to support this effort.

A major source of encouragement is Rotary Ireland whose members have been wonderfully supportive and are keen to support our efforts. Flax Trust, our neighbours on Crumlin Road, has pledged that funds will be available once we are ready to begin.

The Passionist Congregation is the owner of these buildings. Without hesitation, the leadership of the Passionists has indicated that they can be held on a long-term lease. This will enable the formation of a Board of Trustees for the Family Centre. There will also be need of detailed work on how the management of the Centre will be set up.

It is possible that the dream will remain but an aspiration, but not to have attempted to make it a reality would have been a betrayal of the Gospel demand for reconciliation and peace.

The Holy Cross School protest will have had a happy ending the day that children find a place to be safe and loved precisely because they are children beloved by God, and the future of our community.

It is not in my nature to be pessimistic. However, being a realist, I see that the hope of a cross-community centre may fail. If it is not possible at this stage it is my intention to go ahead with the reopening of the Family Centre. All it will mean is that the day of the full sharing has been delayed but not abandoned.

My prayer and hope is that the events of 2001 on Ardoyne Road will be remembered for what they were but also for what they gave birth to. So, what of the future? It is important that we move to the future:

- Being attentive to the hurting places and the silences
- Being attentive to the places of collapse
- Keeping alive the hope of a shared future alive in Northern Ireland

- Being attentive to the new things that are happening – to refugees, asylum seekers, ethnic minorities, gays and lesbians
- Being aware of the importance of people meeting across unexpected lines
- Being a learning community and sharing that learning with others
- Being convinced that out of relationships surprising things happen
- Being attentive to the strangeness of the Gospel and wishing to go on the Way with Jesus, wherever that might take us
- Being attentive to the importance of Christian Community and finding new ways of faith in Northern Ireland where churches are in deep crisis.

The agenda can be spoken in different ways. The outline above gives some idea of what lies ahead. It will not be easy and there is no guarantee that we will succeed. The challenge is to take small steps and retain the humility to retrace our steps when things go wrong.

The walk that became known as the Holy Cross School protest will have been in vain only if we don't take up the journey again towards a new and better future. Some of the children who walked in 2001 are now 15 years of age. It is still too early to tell what the long-term effects will be. The prayer and hope is that the damage will be repaired and that the pain will eventually ease. The love of parents for their children will be a fundamental building block for the future. One day, I hope we can tell the world that the outcome was better than anyone could have imagined.

We have a long way to go. But the late great Archbishop Oscar Romero who was murdered for his beliefs leaves us with a fitting prayer:

It helps now and then to step back
and take the long view.
The Kingdom is not only beyond our efforts,
it is even beyond our vision.
We accomplish in our lifetime only a tiny fraction
of the magnificent enterprise that is God's work.

Nothing we do is complete,
which is another way of saying
that the Kingdom always lies beyond us.
No statement says all that could be said.
No prayer fully expresses our faith.
No confession brings perfection,
no pastoral visit brings wholeness.
No programme accomplishes the Church's mission.
No set of goals and objectives includes everything.
This is what we are about.
We plant the seeds that one day will grow.
We water seeds already planted,
knowing that they hold future promise.
We lay foundations that will need further development.
We provide yeast that produces effects far beyond our capabilities.
We cannot do everything,
and there is a sense of liberation in realising that.
This enables us to do something, and to do it very well.
It may be incomplete, but is a beginning,
a step along the way,
an opportunity for the Lord's grace to enter and do the rest.
We may never see the end results,
but that is the difference between
the master builder and the worker.
We are workers, not master builders,
ministers, not messiahs.
We are prophets of a future not our own. Amen

EPILOGUE

THE JOURNEY OVER the past few years has been one of blessing and grace. It has also had its pain and suffering. In other words, they have been Paschal years. There is something of Calvary but overwhelmed by Resurrection.

Where it will lead is known only to God. Revelation continues in the events as they unfold. It is my hope that Ardoyne and the surrounding area will soon find the path to peace and reconciliation. It is possible and at times seems so breathtakingly close and at others so distant.

The key element is to risk leaving the known land and taking the journey as did Abraham when he left all that was familiar and followed God's call. There is the call to us to take the path of the Exodus and go with Moses to our Pharaohs of today and ask to be set free from slavery and bondage.

'The Truth and Reconciliation Commission' of South Africa may not be capable of being transposed to our situation. Also, we don't have Archbishop Desmond Tutu to lead such a listening body. That said, we must find a way of letting the painful stories and even the hatred be released. Without this, there will be the continuing festering of decades (centuries?) of heartbreak, wounds, resentment and anger. There is among us 'blindness' and 'deafness' that needs to be rescued from the darkness and brought out in the sunshine of daylight. Everyone who wants to tell their story must be heard. It will take real wisdom to design the method of achieving this absolutely necessary next step.

The question often arises as to how these stories would fare with the state justice system. This is where I believe we need to turn to the Gospel and search for the Christ-like way of dealing with this. Murder and the most awful deeds were perpetrated by all sides. Nothing can undo that damage that will live on and on in families. It would be crass, insensitive and inappropriate to gloss over these atrocities and in any way minimise their depravity and evil nature. But if we rely on the state scales of justice, we will continue to fill our prisons. This will, of course, make some people feel good. There are still many Old Testament people around who sincerely believe in 'an eye for an eye and a tooth for a tooth'. Such people see no other way forward and are already in prison themselves.

But there is another way. There is the way of greatness and generosity of spirit. It is the way of forgiveness. It is the option not to lock up prisoners but 'to set prisoners free'. There is scarcely one of us who is not a prisoner in some way or another. We need liberation and healing. The way of forgiveness does not ask us to deny the hurt, the evil perpetrated or the devastation caused. The challenge is to let go of the burden of the past, together, and walk into the brightness of tomorrow. It takes heroism and great strength. It takes the grace of God for the victim to see beyond the terrorist, the bomber or the sniper to the human being that still exists. It is easier to call out 'animal' than to reach out a trembling hand of peace. Behind the most heinous of criminal acts, God still sees someone made in his image and likeness. It is as radical as that.

Equally, the soldier, the police or state agencies that killed or contributed to death and destruction must also be invited to tell their story and face up to what they did. For the Westminster Parliament to pass legislation to prevent such acts from ever being known is a seriously retrograde step. It cuts at the very roots of bringing the conflict to any sort of healing.

It is my prayer that hearts will soften and people will risk moving out of fixed positions, and will find a way out of prison and into the freedom of the children of God. My prayer is that the children of the children of the Holy Cross School protest will never know the pain their parents went through.

Index